Bernard E. Clair and Anthony R. Daniele
are also authors of
LOVE PACT: A LAYMAN'S COMPLETE GUIDE
TO LEGAL LIVING
TOGETHER AGREEMENTS

CONSULTATION WITH A DIVORCE LAWYER

by BERNARD E. CLAIR
and ANTHONY R. DANIELE

A FIRESIDE BOOK
Published by Simon and Schuster   New York

Copyright © 1982 by Bernard E. Clair and Anthony R. Daniele

All rights reserved
including the right of reproduction
in whole or in part in any form
A Fireside Book
Published by Simon and Schuster
A Division of Gulf & Western Corporation
Simon & Schuster Building
Rockefeller Center
1230 Avenue of the Americas
New York, New York 10020

FIRESIDE and colophon are registered trademarks of Simon & Schuster

Designed by Leonard Telesca
Manufactured in the United States of America

Printed and bound by Fairfield Graphics

10 9 8 7 6 5 4 3 2 1

Library of Congress Cataloging in Publication Data
Clair, Bernard E.
   Consultation with a divorce lawyer.

   1. Divorce—Law and legislation—United
States—Miscellanea.   I. Daniele, Anthony R.
II. Title.
KF535.Z9C57   1982   346.7301'66   82–5989
ISBN 0-671-44192-2   347.306166   AACR2

AUTHORS' NOTE

Throughout the book, you will come upon quotations from some of our own cases. In the interests of privacy, the names of the combatants have been changed, although the quote itself is straight from the judge's lips.

ACKNOWLEDGMENTS

In our minds, no book is complete without a specific acknowledgment to those who assisted along the way. Our thanks and appreciation to: Elise and Arnold Goodman, Maureen Heffernan, Richard Huttner, Helena Gorochow, Jeanne Glassman and Evelyn Prasetyo.

CONTENTS

INTRODUCTION

As any person experiencing the divorce process knows, beginning a divorce can be a very frightening and harrowing experience, especially to those entering a divorce with either very little or no knowledge as to what lies ahead. For too long, divorce clients have had to acquire the knowledge of divorce through hearsay, or through their own experiences, not knowing most of the time what will happen next.

Messrs. Clair and Daniele have now given the public their first practical guidebook to the rapidly expanding and challenging field of matrimonial law: *Consultation with a Divorce Lawyer*. The book is indispensable to the novice of divorce procedures; but of no less value to the experienced attorney, who, with increasing frequency, discovers the growing complexity of individuals' financial structures and life styles reflected in the ever-expanding field of divorce law cases he handles.

The book is, in essence, a manual and is indexed for quick, easy and direct reference. *Consultation with a Divorce Lawyer* emphasizes strategy and tactics and offers explicit advice at each stage of the divorce proceedings. Its chapters move from the initial breakup of the marriage to the final settlement, as well as any post-divorce problems that may occur. Messrs. Clair and Daniele consider every matter that may prove significant: choosing the right attorney, protecting the assets of the parties, involving the children, visitation and custody, support, the litigation process, court and out-of-court settlements and post-divorce problems. Above all, the book is crammed with hypothetical questions that clients who are about to embark in the difficult process of divorce ask their attorneys. Although Messrs. Clair and Daniele are New York lawyers, much of the contents of their book has universal application to any prospective divorce client, as well as to matrimonial lawyers, in any of the fifty states.

We are witnessing profound changes in the long-term personal commitment, institutionalized and named marriage. Marriage grew out of society's need to establish a climate to nurture and safeguard its health and vital growth. Society now frankly accepts and often prefers alternatives to traditional marital ties. Marriage, although dignified by tradition, now co-exists with recognized common law obligations, living-together arrangements, changing family life styles and alternative sex roles. Any of these ties or connections may break down and the divorce lawyer must be prepared to harness the legal system to bring equity to persons in situations for which the conventional processes of law do not provide.

For this reason, every prospective divorce client, as well as every attorney, should have a copy of this book; mine is already well thumbed. I'm sure it would have been helpful for some of my clients to have had such a source of information when starting their divorce proceedings.

With Messrs. Clair and Daniele's insights, their keen, searching minds and their rare ability to combine their talents for techniques with methodology, they have given us the practical means to navigate and sound the ever expanding waters of divorce law.

MARVIN M. MITCHELSON

PHASE I:

UNRAVELING

A marriage is coming undone. The realization hurts, and the uncertainties are unsettling. Hard choices lie ahead, decisions forged between conflicting advice and desperate impulses. There are many questions and few answers. Worse still are the sudden emergencies and unanticipated problems, for which there seem to be no solutions. Legal counsel is essential but rarely sought at this early stage; no one even knows a good attorney.

Often lacking immediate access to legal counsel, many persons make critical mistakes that often prove prejudicial to their cases in the long run. The prospective destruction of the marriage is by itself emotionally traumatic, and few are equipped to deal with the legal and financial decisions that must be made from the very beginning. If there are children, the problems grow even more complex.

It is a difficult time to make decisions, and yet it is amazing to whom one will turn for advice. A neighbor, a sister, an uncle, a business associate or a cab driver may be highly sympathetic and understanding, but even if he or she has gone through a divorce, the credentials are wanting. The closer the person is to you and your situation, the more subjectively vindictive his or her suggestions may be. This is not a time for reinforcing your baser impulses—"Throw the bastard out and change the locks." The temptation is great for an emotional release, and a friend's suggestion to go on a spending spree can be most enthusiastically received. Unfortunately, the long-term consequences can prove destructive, preventing a fair and adequate resolution of those property and financial claims that must eventually be resolved as part of the divorce.

This section answers the frequently asked questions and explains the important issues that are encountered at this initial phase of the divorce. Just because the marriage is falling apart does not necessarily mean that everything else has to go with it, and practical guidance is provided covering topics from possession of the home to custody of the children. Finally, suggestions are offered with regard to choosing and retaining an experienced attorney to represent you in the divorce.

Chapter One

BREAKING UP: THE HARD CHOICES

Marriages end in many ways, some slowly, others dramatically. Nevertheless, the process eventually reaches the point where both spouses know it is over. It may be a telephone call, announcing that the last three nights of unexplained absence are only to be interrupted by a visit on Saturday afternoon to pack a suitcase. Maybe it was a quiet conversation over dinner, where he agreed it would be best if she moved back to her mother's with the two children. There are sometimes fights, threats, even physical abuse, and it could be the summoned police officer who suggests that one or the other move out.

Depending on the way the end of the marriage begins, different questions are raised. A husband, for example, comes home late one night from work, discovering that his wife is not home, many of her everyday belongings are missing and three suitcases are gone. Two weeks go by without a word. A co-worker says not to let her back in because she has abandoned him. The confused husband asks, "Do I change the locks?" Before he calls the locksmith, he remembers that there is about $7,500 in a joint savings account, and he begins to wonder what he should do about it.

YOUR HOME

The first area treated in this chapter is the possession and occupancy of the home. Ordinarily it is extremely uncomfortable for estranged spouses to continue living together, so someone has to move out. One frequently does, for emotional rather than practical reasons. Sometimes neither person budges; economic realities and acute housing shortages may make moving impossible. In other instances one spouse is only too happy to leave the other person with the house, mortgage payments and fuel bills. Even if the couple reaches an accommodation—"I'll sleep in the den"—one spouse may later become abusive. Some couples decide it is best to sell the house and split the money, yet for others the issue of ownership itself is disputed.

Our home is in a virtual state of siege, but no one wants to (or can afford to) leave. Can I get him out?

Sometimes. If you can convince the judge that the situation presents a clear and present danger of either serious mental or physical harm, then a court may give you exclusive temporary occupancy of the home until your divorce. This is done by making a pretrial motion or application to the court specifying the reasons for the request.

Must show clear and present danger

Temporary exclusive occupancy is difficult to get without compelling proof. In the eyes of the law, the marital home is a sacred property right, one which is to be enjoyed equally by both spouses and which is not lightly tampered with by the courts. Consequently, most judges are reluctant to oust a spouse unless the other can show real or threatened harm. Even if you come to court with bruises, the court will first have to explore other important factors such as the availability of alternative housing and whether your spouse can afford it, whether there are children involved, how long you have been living together, the length of your marriage and even the timing of your request.

Sacred legal rights

Other factors considered

Herman and Shirley have been married twenty-six years, the last six of which have been pure hell. They live in a condominium apartment that Herman purchased in his own name over fourteen years ago. They both work out of the apartment. He is a math tutor, and she is a freelance clothing designer. Herman thought that once his lawyer started the divorce, getting his wife out of "his" apartment would be a relatively easy task. What he did not expect was that the divorce would drag on for five years, during which time "lines" have been drawn in the apartment, separating the living areas and making a sad mockery of "his" and "hers" towels.

Shirley has steadfastly refused to move out, because she feels that she is entitled to a property interest in the apartment. Also she claims that she cannot afford to go anywhere else. Herman complains that he cannot conduct his tutoring because his wife is abusive to him and his students. Shirley feels that Herman is the abusive one and that his behavior makes it impossible for her to concentrate on her work. Herman's lawyer applied to the court for exclusive occupancy; Shirley's lawyer did the same on her behalf. It was a stalemate. Neither could show to the judge's satisfaction that their situation posed any great threat to either their physical or mental well-being. Moreover, the judge questioned how they could have tolerated this situation for four years before making their requests. The judge ruled that "mere squabbles and intransigence, and even overt hatred, is not alone sufficient grounds for the granting of temporary occupancy in favor of one spouse as against the other without a showing of dire physical or emotional stress."

The longer the marriage and the longer the couple has stayed together under such debilitating conditions the less likely the judge will award exclusive occupancy. He or she will feel that if you have been living together that long it really cannot be as bad as you claim. Most will defer the decision as to who ultimately gets the home to the judge conducting the divorce trial, unless there is a serious threat of harm that requires earlier judicial intervention.

I think I can get exclusive temporary occupancy of my home. How can I go about doing it?

Most states have a procedure whereby your lawyer can make an application or *motion* to the court for an interim decision, or, as lawyers like to say, "temporary relief." The application need not be confined to just one request, and a typical pretrial motion will contain requests affecting property rights, alimony, child support and even counsel fees.

Temporary motions for pretrial relief

The motion or application is usually made by submitting to the court sworn affidavits alleging the various conditions that necessitate the request. Sometimes the lawyers argue their respective cases before the judge, and sometimes the judge directs that a hearing (a mini-trial) be held immediately on those issues. One caveat: in congested urban courts a judge's decision may not be rendered for weeks, or even months. Nevertheless, pretrial motions are often the only shot you have, particularly when you consider that it is not uncommon for bitterly contested divorces to take more than a year to get to trial and

Applying a Band-aid

be finally resolved. Finally, always keep in mind that the relief you get is temporary; it will only last until the parties reach a settlement or the trial judge makes his or her final decision.

She walks out and says that she is never coming back. A few days pass and still no word. Do I change the locks?

No. As attorneys, we rarely counsel our clients to change locks, even though that is something that every friend, neighbor and relative will recommend. Unless there is a real and serious danger of physical harm or theft, the status quo should be preserved. Just because she walked out of the house does not mean that she has relinquished all of her rights as your wife. These will be determined some day by a judge, not a locksmith.

Judge vs. locksmith

My husband has just told me that if I don't give him the divorce he is going to stop paying the mortgage and force the bank to foreclose on our home. Can he do it?

He can try, but if you act quickly he will not succeed. Once again you have the right to make a pretrial motion or application. If you can show the court that your husband had been paying the mortgage and all of the other carrying charges on the home, chances are very good that the court will direct him to continue paying until the issues of ownership and support can be decided at trial.

Court may order payments to continue

This type of economic threat is common, and judges see through it. Of course, make sure that you are not "crying wolf." Just because your husband threatened does not mean that he will go through with his threat. At the same time, do not wait until the sheriff is auctioning off your house. If a mortgage payment is missed, most banks will be understanding and reluctant to do anything once they are informed that there is a matrimonial dispute. We have found that sending a letter to the bank often helps until the slow wheels of justice can intervene.

Economic blackmail

Thrifty Savings and Loan Association
14 West Main Street
Elks Rapids, Michigan 49629

Re: Mortgage Account No. 003-4167-34

Sample letter to bank

Dear Sir/Madam:

Please be advised that I am a joint title owner of the premises at 40 Metalock Lane, Elks Rapids. My husband has threatened to withhold the monthly mortgage payments due under the above-referenced mortgage.

Please be further advised that we are currently in the midst of a divorce action, and that my attorney will be proceeding immediately with an application to the court directing that my husband continue making said payments. In the interim, I would appreciate your forebearance and communication with respect to any default on the mortgage.

My attorney will forward to you a copy of the court's decision immediately upon our receipt of same.

Thank you for your cooperation and courtesies.

Very truly yours,
Linda Jacoby

She's left me the apartment but her name was always on the lease. Now the landlord says that I have no right to be there. He wants me out immediately. Can he do it?

Probably not. In most states a lease extends to family members. As long as you remain married, you have a right to be there. Of course, after the divorce, the situation may change, but it is too soon to worry about that now. Sometimes a landlord will request that you sign a new lease, but this is for his protection and has nothing to do with your divorce. *Family members protected*

Since the blow-out, her mother and father have virtually moved into my house. Is there any legal way to get them out?

Yes. Your home is *your* castle, not theirs. Again a pretrial motion or application can be used to limit the time that the in-laws visit. In this situation, you do not really even have to show that you are suffering extreme mental or physical distress, for most judges will realize that the continued presence of one spouse's parents is potentially abusive and destabilizing. *Protection from over-zealous in-laws*

A husband we represented faced exactly this situation. His wife's parents were there ostensibly for their daughter's protection. However, the wife was unable to show protection was indeed necessary, and the husband's request to limit the parents' visitation resulted in this order: "The wife is directed not to permit her parents to remain in the marital premises between the hours of 8:00 P.M. and 9:00 A.M. the following morning."

We both agreed to a trial separation and to selling our jointly owned home, but we can't seem to agree on the selling price. Any suggestions?

Assuming you are both serious about selling the house, which would mean that you would want the best possible price and are not playing games with one another, any impasse can be resolved by using the same procedure that lawyers frequently incorporate in written separation agreements. What is done is this: each person picks his or her own broker. Each broker then sets a price. If the prices are different but not more than $10,000 apart, an average is taken, and that becomes the agreed-upon selling price. If the price is more than $10,000 apart, the two brokers pick a third broker, who makes the final and binding determination.

Payment of closing costs

It is also a good idea to discuss who will be responsible for the various selling costs, such as commissions, transfer taxes, attorneys' fees and other closing costs. Usually both agree to split them evenly, but there may be a reason why you will want this done differently in your case. At any rate, the idea is to discuss it at the beginning, and not fight over it when the deed is about to be signed.

My husband says that because his name is on the deed the house is his and that if he wants to sell it I can't stop him. Is he right?

May have marital interest or right to exclusive occupancy

Not necessarily. Depending upon the matrimonial laws in your state, you may have a legal claim of ownership of the house. Furthermore, most courts have power, depending upon the circumstances, to make an award of temporary occupancy, so even if your husband owns the house, he would not be able to sell it as long as such an order is in effect.

Claiming ownership under divorce laws

The vast majority of states today are either *community property* or *equitable distribution* jurisdictions. This means that a spouse can make a claim against any property that was acquired *during* the marriage. The only difference is that in community property states both spouses would ordinarily be given an equal share, while in the equitable distribution states the property is divided in a way that the court determines is fair and reasonable under the particular circumstances of the case.

Prior acquisitions and gifts exempt

Remember that the matrimonial laws can only affect property that was acquired during the marriage. Therefore, if your husband owned the house before the marriage, it is unlikely that you would be able to make a matrimonial claim on the property. Moreover, certain acquisitions during the marriage are also exempt from matrimonial laws in most states. For example, if your father-in-law either gave your husband the house or left it to him in his will, it is unlikely that you would be entitled to any share of the house. However, you still may be entitled to an order of exclusive occupancy.

There are a handful of states that are still so-called *title* jurisdictions. This means that if the property is solely in your husband's name, it is considered his, and the title cannot be affected under the matrimonial laws. However, in some instances, you may be able to make a claim for a *constructive trust*. This is a very technical form of relief, and you should really consult with an attorney to determine whether you are entitled to make such a claim. In the meantime, there is still something you can do to prevent the sale of the house. You may commence a preliminary proceeding for a court order that will give you temporary occupancy and at the same time prevent your husband from consummating a sale of the home. *Deed controls in title states* *Constructive trusts*

An order of temporary occupancy is available in family and matrimonial courts in virtually every state. What it does is maintain the status quo until claims of ownership can be determined either under your state's matrimonial laws or by instituting an action for a constructive trust. Such orders are especially appropriate when there are children involved, because the court does not want the lives and surroundings of the children unnecessarily disturbed until a final determination can be made. Even if there are no children, if you demonstrate to the court compelling circumstances, such as the inability to find or afford alternative accommodations until your claim is litigated, it is very likely that you will obtain an order of temporary occupancy. This is especially true if you have been married for a long time and are not working. This order may also require that your husband continue to pay the carrying charges on the house during the pendency of the divorce action. *Temporary order of exclusive occupancy* *Paying carrying charges*

Please refer to the appendix to determine whether your state is a title, community property or equitable distribution jurisdiction. *See Appendix*

I bought the co-op before I knew him; the property is in my name alone. I want the miserable skunk out now. Can I do it?

As we have already seen, the title document is not controlling in equitable distribution or community property states. Your husband may have rights to the cooperative apartment even though it is solely in your name. Therefore no judge is going to summarily eject your husband until his rights in the co-op can be fully determined. Of course, as we have already seen, if you can show the court that his presence constitutes a clear and present danger to your emotional or physical safety, then it is possible to get a temporary order of exclusive occupancy, which will keep him out and leave the final property determination to the trial judge.

Title document usually not controlling

Nothing in the law is absolutely certain, and every once in a while there is an unusual case that produces unusual results. Jerry and Beth had been married for five years when they broke up and sold their house. Beth moved into the city and used her share of the profits to buy a one-bedroom cooperative apartment. Jerry's investments were not so prudent; most of his money disappeared at the race track. A few years went by, and neither took any affirmative legal action to get a divorce. Jerry showed up one day begging for a second chance, and Beth made her second mistake—she let him move in.

The case of the forgiving spouse

It did not take more than four months for the old troubles to resurface, but this time Jerry refused to get out, claiming that under the divorce laws the co-op was half his. Dreaming of another big daily double, he told Beth that they should sell the co-op and split the money again. Beth was not about to make a third mistake. She went to a lawyer, started a divorce action and made an immediate motion to eject her husband.

The court held that, while ordinarily Beth would lack grounds for temporary exclusive occupancy, in this situation Jerry had no right to stay in the apartment because it was not really the marital premises. The judge pointed out that the parties had already divided and distributed their interests in the marital home when it was sold, and that Beth was free to do whatever she wanted with her share. The co-op that Beth purchased in her own name with her own money was therefore not marital property. The judge said that allowing Jerry to move in was a good-faith attempt at reconciliation, for which she should not be penalized by losing any ownership interest in her apartment. Although the judge did not say so, it was clear that in the intervening years Jerry had gone from faithful husband to unwelcomed house-guest.

He admits that the home is in my name, but reminds me that he has been paying the mortgage and taxes since the marriage. He claims to be an equal owner because of his contributions. Is he correct?

This is a complex question, but remember that, except in those title jurisdiction states, a court is not going to be restricted merely by whose name is on the deed. There are many more important factors. For example, who paid for the house? Did you? Or was it from joint funds? How long has your hus- *Marital prop-* band been paying the carrying charges? There is a big differ- *erty inquiries* ence between paying for two months or paying for twenty years. There is no question that if the property was purchased during the marriage with marital funds your husband is entitled to an interest, equal in community property states and proportionate in equitable distribution states.

Yes, I understand that. But what if the house was left me by my aunt?

In virtually every state there is an exclusion for property that you acquire as a gift or by inheritance. Such items fall outside of the umbrella of "marital property." However, nothing is *Inheritance* black and white. For example, your husband may be able to *excepted* prove that you gratuitously gave him an interest in the house during the marriage, or he may be able to show that due to his efforts or expenditures the value of the house has appreciated, thereby entitling him to share in any profits.

Well, if his paying the mortgage is only one factor that the court will consider in determining ownership, do I have to give him back the money?

The court can look at your husband's payments in two ways. First, they can be considered an element of support, and therefore he will not be given any credit for the payments he made. Second, they can be viewed as a loan, and the court will rule that he is entitled to a credit for such payments upon the sale of the house, or sometimes even before. Lawyers call this an *Mortgage* "amortization credit," which means that your husband would *credits* be entitled to recoup that portion of his mortgage payments that was applied to the reduction of principal, but not interest. Each situation is different, and there is no way to predict which way the court will go.

If any general rule can be made, it is that if the court finds that the husband has an ownership interest in the house, he will not receive a credit for the mortgage payments previously paid. However, if the wife is awarded total ownership of the house, then it is much more likely that the husband will be able to get back some of his money.

YOUR POSSESSIONS

Most matrimonial attorneys can relate at least one story in which an otherwise amicable divorce settlement disintegrated because of a dispute over the Sinatra record collection, or something like it. Couples often reach agreement with little rancor on such important issues as custody, child support, alimony and visitation schedules. Then, mysteriously, without apparent reason, a hard-line approach is taken by one or both over how they will divide the "things" accumulated during the marriage.

We have all experienced an attachment for an item that goes well beyond its actual value. Such attachments are often based on emotion and sentiment, which become particularly acute during the dissolution of a relationship. Anger, power trips and destructive bitterness find fertile ground during this agonizing time, and it is a rare individual indeed who does not have to fight to keep perspective. Sadly, many do not succeed. Obviously, arrangements and compromises must be reached—it is impossible to cut the television or car in half.

What is marital property?

Marital property is a term used in community property and equitable distribution states. New York's definition is typical: *marital property* means all property acquired by either or both spouses during the marriage and before the signing of a separation agreement or the commencement of a divorce, regardless of the name in which the property is held. In other words, it is anything that you acquire during your marriage, subject to certain exceptions discussed below.

Marital property defined

Marital property does not include *separate property,* which is defined as (1) property acquired before the marriage or acquired by inheritance or gift from someone other than the spouse; (2) personal injury awards (e.g., from an automobile accident lawsuit); (3) property acquired in exchange for separate property, not including any appreciation that is due partly to the other spouse's contributions or efforts; and (4) any prop-

Separate property excluded

erty that the parties designate in a prenuptial agreement as separate property.

So what is the importance of marital property?
This is the pie that gets divided in the divorce. The more you *Marital pie* can put in the pie, the bigger your piece.

Before our marriage my husband purchased a valuable painting, which is now worth about $50,000. He always proudly pointed to it and said, "Honey, that's our retirement fund." Now that we're getting divorced, his lawyer insists that the painting is separate property and that I have no interest in it. What happened to my share of the retirement fund?
This is how a divorce can suddenly grow complex. Yes, your husband bought the painting before the marriage, and it certainly looks like it would be separate property. However, there is another layer of investigation. His statements can *Lines may be-* be construed by a court as his having made a gift of the *come blurred* painting to you. In such a case you would be entitled to an interest in it. Unfortunately, this is not as simple as it may first appear.

What do you mean it's not simple? He said it, didn't he?
Yes, he may have said it, but you will have to prove that he did. Proof in a divorce trial is elusive, coming down frequently to one person's word against another's. The judge may or may *Proof prob-* not believe you. Of course, if your husband made the statement *lems* before witnesses at a cocktail party, you have a much stronger case. Why don't you start calling up a few friends and relatives? They may remember some circumstances that buttress your position.

Let's assume that the judge believes me and gives me an interest in the painting. What happens? Do we take out the scissors?
The painting would have to be appraised. After the court determines the percentage of your interest, a provision will be made whereby the painting is either sold or your husband buys *Buy-out* out your share—or you buy his share. The ultimate resolution *agreements* depends on the finances of the parties.

What is community property?
Community property is another term for marital property. It *Equal owner-* is the way that community property jurisdictions define "the *ship*

marital pie." The parties are presumed to own community property equally in those states.

Community property defined

California's definition is typical. All real estate located in the state and all personal property wherever located that is acquired during the marriage by either spouse while living in California is community property.

There are several recognized exceptions. The property must be acquired while the parties are living together as husband and wife; if they have separated, property acquired thereafter is deemed the separate property of the spouse acquiring it.

Some exceptions

Real estate located outside of California is not deemed community property. There are also some technical exceptions for real estate acquired in the wife's sole name prior to 1975, which may not qualify as community property. Your attorney will undoubtedly be able to guide you through your state's community property laws.

He is threatening to sell the family car, leaving me no means of transportation. Can he do it?

If a car is solely in his name, he can sell it without your permission, but you may be able to go to court to stop him. Judges try to preserve the status quo during the long months before the divorce trial. Therefore, if you can show that you really need the car and have always used it for such purposes as commuting to work or picking up the kids from school, and that his action seems to be nothing more than a form of harassment or vindictiveness, the odds are pretty much in your favor that the court will prohibit your husband from selling the car until the divorce.

Automobile may be a necessity

What if he has already sold it? What can I do?

If you can convince the court that the use of an automobile is necessary, a judge may require that your husband incur the expenses of either renting or purchasing another car for your benefit. Your attorney must make a pretrial motion or application setting forth the details of your husband's conduct and your previous use of the automobile. A car is a virtual necessity in many parts of the country, and access to one may be considered a proper element of temporary support.

Aspect of support

There is also another consideration that becomes important. Did your husband really sell the car, or was it a fraudulent transfer, perhaps to a relative? If the court finds that the sale was phony—in other words, your husband did not receive the

Fraudulent conveyance

true market value of the car—it has the power to take the car back from any purchaser who is aware that the transaction was fraudulent. In such a case, you may be able to get back the old jalopy.

Courts will always closely scrutinize any transfers of property made during the pendency of a divorce action. There is always the suspicion that one person may be selfishly trying to scoop away some of the marital pie before a judge has had the opportunity to cut it.

Close scrutiny

My husband coolly informs me that all the furniture is his because he bought it. I say that I have an equal right to it. Who's correct?

The first thing you must ask yourself is when your husband purchased the furniture. If he bought it before the marriage, it is separate property, and you will get none of it. On the other hand, if the furniture was purchased during the marriage, you may have an interest in the various items, unless you reside in a title jurisdiction state. (See Appendix.)

Determining marital property

Assuming the furniture was purchased during the marriage and you do not live in a title state, the next issue is to determine what portion of the furniture is yours. In community property states, the furniture gets divided equally according to value; in equitable distribution states, a judge will award you a certain percentage, which varies according to the circumstances of your marriage.

Your share

We both have keys to the safe deposit box at the bank. My father tells me to go to the bank and "clean it out." I know it may be wrong, but my friend who has just gone through a divorce herself says that it is done all the time and that there's nothing anyone can do about it. Is this good advice?

No. Raiding the safe deposit box may very well be an example of short-term agony. Taking what is not yours is nothing but stealing, and it is not a recommended preliminary step in your divorce action.

Don't raid

Your conduct may be deemed by the judge to be tantamount to conversion, which is a non-criminal form of stealing. At the divorce trial, your husband will be entitled to offer evidence of your raid of the safe deposit box, and the judge will have the discretion to make you give the property back or pay your husband its value. More importantly, since so many factors go into property awards in divorce, evidence of your being "the

Stealing

Court will draw negative inferences

bad guy" certainly cannot help your cause. In fact, several states require judges to take into account any such wrongful depletion of marital assets in making their property determination awards.

Yes, I understand this, but my reason for wanting to empty the box is that I'm afraid that my husband will do it anyway. How can I otherwise protect myself?

If you have a legitimate fear that your husband is going to take the money and run, there is a way to protect yourself without appearing to be at fault.

Open new safe deposit box

We counsel our clients in such a situation to visit the safe deposit box as quickly as possible. Once there, we instruct him or her to make a detailed, written inventory of the box's contents. The contents are then emptied from the box and placed in another one in the same bank that has been leased solely in the client's name. Then the client is told to deliver the key to the new safe deposit box along with the inventory to us. We immediately write the other attorney and advise him or her of our client's actions, enclosing with the letter a copy of the inventory.

Protecting status quo

We have found that this procedure, although imperfect, tends to protect the status quo. The couple's assets remain intact and available until the attorneys or the court can fashion a suitable solution.

I have come home early from work, and there is a moving van in the driveway, men struggling with our piano and my wife yelling out instructions. What do I do?

Remain calm

The first thing to do is remain calm. Remember, the moving men are not co-conspirators with your wife, and they have no idea that they are getting involved in a marital dispute, which is the last thing they desire. Approach them and explain the situation and the fact that your wife does not have authority to remove any of the furniture or property from the home. Usually that is enough for them to start unloading the truck. However, if they ignore you or say that it is not their problem, the next step is to record as much information as you can—the name of the moving company, the license plate number of the truck, the names of the movers. The police may also be of some assistance. Another good idea is to call the moving company yourself and explain the situation. Probably reluctant to get involved in any lawsuit, the moving company may direct its

Explain existence of divorce action

men to stop their activities immediately and return the items to the house.

Finally, do not despair if nothing works and you find yourself standing on the sidewalk waving goodbye to your cherished possessions. If you have read this far, you have already seen that there are ways to have your wife account for her misdeeds. Her immediate gratification may prove to be a long-term heartache later.

We've already agreed to a fifty-fifty split of the property. But how do you divide a television in half? I know compromises have to be reached, but can you give me any guidance?

If you already realize that there can be problems, you are more than halfway there. Property division is one of the thorniest issues that any couple can face, even if they have already decided that everything will be divided equally. You can be sure that there are always one or two things that both want which do not come neatly apart at the seams. There has to be a spirit of cooperation; maybe you will give up the Waterford crystal in exchange for the Sony. *Use common sense*

Harry and Gilda were doing great until it came down to the nitty gritty. They had agreed that he would get the den furniture and that she would get the bedroom set. No one wanted the living room furniture, which would be sold and the money divided equally. They had more or less been guiding themselves by monetary value, striving to keep the dollar amount as equal as they could. All was going well until it came to the photo album of their vacations. *Bargaining in good faith*

"I took most of those pictures, so they should be mine," Harry said.

"I picked the vacation spots, and those pictures are my memories too," Gilda answered.

"Well, suppose you take the pictures from Morocco and I'll take the shots of Disney World." *Try creative approaches*

"But the kids are in the Disney World pictures."

A few moments passed, and then Harry had the idea of the century.

"Wait a minute. Why don't I run all the negatives down to Fotomat and have duplicate prints made? You can even keep the album."

This was an obvious solution, but in their overwrought states, Harry and Gilda had almost missed it—a common enough occurrence when spouses allow themselves to be drawn into an emotional quagmire.

The next hurdle was the first edition of *Treasure Island.* What was to be done with that? They discovered it in a small bookstore in south London on their honeymoon, and it had been gathering dust on the shelf for years. But now, faced with the prospect of giving it up, each wanted it more than anything. The answer did not come easily, and almost everything they had already agreed to began to unravel. In fact, it was not until two days later that Gilda came up with the idea of making a gift of the book to their son Mark when he graduated from college in two years. In the meantime, Harry would hold onto the book.

Steve and Sally were not so fortunate. After months of haggling, the only agreement they had reached was that both should have their own clothes and half of the towels. The problem was really the Hummel collection. Sally had always loved them, and in fact for years Steve had wanted to get rid of them. But now he was not going to allow her to have her way, so he insisted that they be divided equally. Three years later, that is exactly what the judge ordered. By that time, neither really cared.

These are nice stories, but how do they help me?

No story or lawyer can help unless you really try to help yourself first. You must realize that marital property is an extremely sensitive topic, and it often does not divide easily. Desire for a particular item is more often anchored in emotion and nostalgia than in its monetary value. It is important for you to isolate your considerations and motives. Is your desire based on one-upmanship? Vindictiveness? Power? Is the item really worth fighting for? When you allow your motives to become confused, no solutions will be reached, and you may soon find yourselves in the same position as Steve and Sally. Be creative; think of alternatives. Leave yourself open to compromise. You both have it within your power to save one another from endless hours of emotionally debilitating agony. If you wait for the judge to decide, the court's property division will more times than not be arbitrary, pleasing no one.

Analyze your motives

I have just come back from a business trip and discovered that the bedroom and living room sets are gone. My husband, with a

*smirk on his face, informs me that "we've been robbed." Do I
have any recourse?*

You do if you can prove that he is lying. Actually, this is a
lot easier than it sounds. First, take a moment to accurately
determine for yourself the missing items. Next, find out from
your husband if he has reported the "theft" to the police. If he
says yes, then check with the police and obtain a copy of their *Playing detec-*
report. If your husband has not filed a robbery report, this fact *tive*
alone may hold you in good stead later when your lawyer attempts to prove your husband's duplicity.

Assuming the report has been filed, a copy will provide you
with details of the alleged robbery. An obvious question to ask
is why only the bedroom and living room furniture was stolen.
What kind of burglar hits only sofas and beds? Why weren't
your jewelry, cash and watches touched? Now that you are
playing detective, do not let up. Redouble your efforts. Do any
neighbors remember a moving van in the driveway? Does your
husband have a place to store the furniture?

The idea is to gather evidence that shows the absurdity of
your husband's claim. For the most part, it has been our experience that divorce judges are far from naive; they have been
there before. Consequently, they are very aware that many *Gathering evi-*
spouses will conduct themselves in highly questionable ways *dence of*
when it comes to the issues that often surface during a marital *spouse's du-*
dispute. *plicity*

*The antique china has been in my family forever. He insists
that it is half his. Is he right?*

No. Your china is a perfect example of separate property, *Separate*
something which you had before the marriage or which was *property*
given to you by your family.

*My husband says that because we're planning to file for divorce
he is entitled to the return of my engagement ring. I say no. Who
is right?*

You are. It has long been held by our courts that an engagement ring is a gift in comtemplation of marriage. Once the *Gift in con-*
marriage takes place, it is yours forever. *templation of*
Do not be surprised if your husband asks for the ring. You *marriage*
may be surprised to learn how often this happens, and you
would be even more surprised to learn how many wives decide
to turn the ring over. Many feel that without the marriage the

ring has no value and no longer wish to wear a symbol of that union. So just because the ring is legally yours, you may consider whether you want your husband to have it anyway.

My wife says that if we can't agree on who gets the sailboat, the court can force us to sell it. Is she correct?

Yes. If the court decides that the sailboat is marital property, it will order a division. Obviously the boat cannot be cut in half, so if the parties cannot decide between themselves, there will be a court-ordered sale. This is something that should be avoided at all costs, because everyone loses. Judicial sales never bring the same amount of money that regular sales do; moreover, there are certain costs and expenses in connection with these sales, such as sheriff's fees and auction expenses, that come right off the top. The best way is to arrange for one spouse to buy out the other's share after having the boat valuated, or to put an ad in the paper, sell the boat and divide the money.

Judicial sale brings less profit

YOUR MONEY

Most couples have checking and savings accounts, as well as immediate sources of credit, such as charge accounts, travel cards, credit cards and overdraft privileges. It is essential that neither person commit economic suicide, just as it is important that a dependent spouse maintain access to these sources of funds.

As a rule, a marriage break-up is unfortunately not the occasion when financial affairs can be discussed calmly. Very often there is an unwarranted grab for whatever is lying around by the person closest to it. This should be prevented, ideally by attempting some reasonable discussions, but such accommodations are sadly the exception rather than the rule. Judy and Steve Robbins certainly discovered this within a week after he stormed angrily out of the house.

Like many middle-income couples, Judy and Steve had not managed to accumulate much savings. Except for food, nearly everything was bought on credit. Thus Steve was not too concerned that his wife had the savings passbook, and the $238.47 that went along with it. He knew he could get a cash advance on his MasterCard to cover the first month's rent and security deposit on the apartment he was taking across town. Judy had yet to buy the kids' clothes for the new school year; unfortunately, she had put this off for a few weeks because of her marital difficulties. On the same morning that she got a call from Steve notifying her of his new address, she took Amy and Vanessa to The Kid Shoppe. With a careful eye on the price tags, she selected enough items to get them through the fall.

Judy brought the items to the cashier, and the kids went outside to play. She handed the woman Steve's duplicate MasterCard. With a nod and a smile, the cashier slipped the card into the side of a cash register, which looked more like a leftover prop from *Star Wars*. She pressed a few keys and waited. A red indicator light appeared on her console, and she pressed a few more keys. A few seconds later an L.E.D. readout appeared on the screen.

"I'm sorry, ma'am, but according to this you are already over the credit line for that card," she said politely, almost whispering. "Do you have any other cards?"

Judy handed her the Visa. The same routine was repeated. So were the results. The cashier apologetically told Judy that unless she had cash for the clothes, she could not have them; no, the store did not accept personal checks. The cash Judy had was not enough, and she needed that anyway for tonight's dinner.

"There must be some mistake," she said in as convincing a voice as she could muster. "I'll check with my husband."

Judy did manage to get through to Steve later in the afternoon. They both discovered that through a combination of need and greed, along with some poor financial planning, they had managed to use up virtually all their sources of ready cash and credit. Many couples quickly find themselves in the same situation and have important questions.

What do I do about our joint credit cards? Can I protect myself from having to pay for her spending spree?

Divorce courts are filled with stories of wives and husbands who go about abusing their credit cards as soon as the marriage begins to fall apart. This is just another example of the "grab-as-much-as-you-can" syndrome. Ideally, everything will be resolved after the trial, but in the meantime there are certain measures that you can take.

Never lose sight of the fact that use of joint credit cards *Joint credit* makes you liable to the credit card company for all purchases, *card liability*

Two-step approach: telephone and write

whether you make them or not. Therefore it is important that you notify the company immediately and close the account. This can readily be done in situations where the card was obtained on your credit and your wife was given a supplemental card. We recommend a two-step approach: telephoning and a follow-up letter. Most credit card companies have a toll-free number that you can use to contact them in situations such as this. Your letter can read as follows:

Ready Credit Card Company
P.O. Box 3580
Sioux Falls, SD 57101

Sample letter to credit card company

Re: Termination of Account No. 416-5278-3006-009

Gentlemen:

Pursuant to my telephone conversation of today, please be advised that the above-referenced account is to be closed immediately and a final bill rendered in connection with same.

I will not be responsible for any charges made upon said account subsequent to the date hereof. Thank you for your immediate attention.

Yours truly,
Donald
Debtor

Make it a short, concise letter—exactly the way all letters to credit card companies should be. We're not entirely sure, but we suspect that they are read by computers with limited vocabulary and patience.

Should I withdraw the entire $7,500 that my wife and I have in a joint savings account?

No. Unless there is a real and immediate emergency that requires withdrawing all the money, the account should be left alone and should continue to be maintained jointly until a settlement or judicial determination is reached. Only something that would require unilateral action, such as a medical emergency for one of the children, warrants cleaning out the account.

Equal ownership presumed

Joint accounts create a presumption of equal ownership and control of the money. Although each person actually owns half, he or she may withdraw the entire amount. However, by so doing, he or she may later be held liable for the other spouse's share. Technically it is a form of stealing, although we cannot recall anyone going to jail for it recently. Nevertheless, because your spouse may choose to ignore this and exercise his or her control over the money by withdrawing it completely, something must be done.

The best precaution to take until you are able to obtain specific legal advice is to contact the bank and put a "hold" on the account. Of course, this means that neither person may be able to touch the money until the "hold" is suspended, but in the in- *Place a* terim it prevents any wrongful, and often wasteful, use of the *"hold" on the* money. Most states permit either person to place it verbally on *account* the telephone. Some banking regulations, however, require a formal writing. Therefore you should telephone an officer at the branch where the account is maintained to ascertain what is required. If he or she replies that the bank will need written authorization, the following form letter may be used:

Thrifty Savings & Loan Association
14 West Main Street
Lynn, Mass. 01905
Re: Savings Account 0003-0000-00 in the joint names of: John
    T. Deposit and/or Mary I. Deposit

Gentlemen:

Please be advised that as an authorized signator of the above-referenced account, I hereby demand that all with- *Sample letter* drawals of both principal and interest from said account be re- *to bank* strained and suspended for a period of thirty (30) days, unless notified otherwise by me or my attorneys.

Please be further advised that should any withdrawals be authorized during this period I will hold your institution liable for any such sums, including interest thereon.

Very truly yours,
Mary I. Deposit

What do I do if my husband has already cleaned out our joint savings account?

Not much. Unless the bank had previously received a "hold" notice, as appears above, it cannot be held responsible for permitting your husband to withdraw the funds. Of course, this does not mean that the money is lost forever. Your attor- *Later reim-* ney will undoubtedly include the lost funds as part of your *bursement* marital claim against your husband. Your husband will have to account for these funds at some point and reimburse you directly for your marital share.

Can I have the bank cancel the overdraft privileges on our joint account?

Joint control means no unilateral action

No. Both you and your wife have equal control over the joint checking account. The same holds true for the overdraft privileges, whereby you can write a check for more money than you have in the account up to a designated credit limit. Neither of you can close the account or cancel the overdraft privileges without the consent of the other, according to banking regulations in most states.

Seek voluntary consent

We suggest that you seek your wife's voluntary consent—directly or through your attorneys, depending upon your relationship. As you are *both* liable for any overdrafts, which are really just loans by the bank at high interest rates, any abuse by your wife adversely affects her as well. Moreover, a judge may ultimately reduce an alimony or maintenance award to your wife by the amount necessary to repay the bank.

My wife refuses to sign a form that will permit the bank to "rollover" our joint $10,000 CD. What can I do?

Either may "rollover"

In most states, one can renew or "rollover" a joint certificate of deposit with the signature of either depositor. We suggest you contact the bank and obtain the necessary forms. Renewing a CD is an advisable and prudent method of preserving the parties' financial status quo during the divorce.

Can I get a $500 cash advance on his credit card?

Obtaining cash for necessities

If you are entitled to use the credit card and the company offers cash advances, you certainly may go ahead and obtain the money. However, be sure it is for a good reason. If you need the money to meet a certain expense for the upkeep of the house, clothing for the children, food money, medical and pharmacy bills or any other necessity, and your husband refuses to provide you with the money, this is certainly a quick way to obtain the cash. Your actions should not be held against you later. On the other hand, if you want the money for a weekend in Atlantic City, a new coat that you do not really need or any other frivolity, then you act at your own risk.

Conduct during early stages of divorce closely scrutinized

This is as good a time as any to point out that a court will ordinarily scrutinize your conduct during the early stages of the divorce more closely than at any other period. Your actions during this crucial time will often have great bearing on the court's ultimate decision affecting property distribution and your other rights. Judges are human, and even if your state's laws do not expressly require them to take into account such wasteful actions, they cannot help but remember your conduct when it comes time to divide marital property, grant maintenance and fix child support.

Things have been pretty bad for about a month. When I got the phone bill I saw that my wife had apparently been seeking advice from every person she has ever known. Do I have to keep paying for all of these long distance calls? How can I protect myself from further abuses?

You cannot deny your wife access to the telephone, but you may be able to curtail any excessive use. If you feel that these phone bills will cause serious financial setbacks for you, you can apply to the court for an order making your wife responsible for her own toll calls. Otherwise, you can wait for the trial, and request a ruling then that your wife should be held re- *Retroactive* troactively responsible for those excessive costs. Perhaps the *rulings* best thing to do first is to talk to her and have her realize that imposing such needless financial burdens on you will do her no good, because there will only be less money left to provide for her real needs.

YOUR SAFETY

None of the topics covered in this chapter are as important as safety to those unfortunate spouses who find themselves in a deteriorating situation where their physical security, and perhaps their children's, is endangered. Living under such conditions quickly becomes unbearable, if not outright dangerous, and there is no reason why anyone should have to tolerate it. Fortunately, every state has a procedure whereby a threatened spouse can alleviate the situation, going as far in some instances as legally ejecting or even imprisoning an abusive spouse.

Last night my husband became verbally abusive and took a swing at me. I called the police, but when they came and learned that it was "a marital dispute" they told me that there was nothing they could do. Is this always the case?

Unfortunately, when it comes to marital disputes, the police are loath to interfere. There is a favored, if not always articulated, policy that what goes on in the home is the couple's busi- *Police have* ness, and no one else's. This is especially true if there are no *an "off* signs of physical assault. Many states are just beginning to *limits" policy* change their laws so that a threatened spouse can invoke the sanctions of the criminal court system, but in most states these disputes are referred to family courts. However, this does not mean that you are defenseless. You can go to a family court, or some other similar court in your state, and obtain what is called an *order of protection*.

What is an order of protection?

Order of protection defined

This is a court order prohibiting your spouse from certain specified actions, including verbal abuse, threats and physical assaults. This order is not granted lightly, because if your husband disobeys it he may very well wind up in jail. Moreover, the police are more likely to take affirmative action when there is an order of protection, which signals that a judge has already determined that there is a threatening situation. Many states, in fact, require that the court file a copy of the order with the local police or sheriff. Texas, in its recent Protection of the Family Act, mandates that each law enforcement department establish procedures to provide the names of persons protected by such orders to officers responding to calls.

How can I get one?

Obtaining an order of protection

Every state has its own procedure, so it is impossible to outline those steps. Generally you make an application, usually written, in the court in your area that has jurisdiction over such family matters. The application should contain concise information about the threatening or dangerous situation. Usually within ten days a writ or summons is then served on (delivered to) your spouse, giving notice of the time, date and place of the court hearing on your application for an order of protection.

Temporary order of protection

If your situation is perilous, you should request a *temporary* order of protection, which most states permit. The court will grant such an order, which offers protection immediately and stays in effect until the time of the hearing, if your application contains information that there is a clear and present danger of violence. The temporary order of protection is made without notice to your spouse and without a hearing, and it may contain restrictions similar to a permanent order. It is usually served on him or her with the summons or writ that contains notice of the hearing for the permanent order.

Must show that your situation is dangerous

Once a court mechanism is set in motion, your spouse will have an opportunity to refute your charges at a hearing. You must provide the court with satisfactory proof at the hearing that your situation is dangerous. Nothing is more convincing than the existence of a bruise or a hospital record. Also, you can use testimony from friends or relatives who have witnessed certain incidents. Some judges require nothing more than being shown that there is a real threat of harm, and they will give you an order of protection if your story is convincing enough. After the judge has heard both sides he will decide whether to issue a *permanent* order of protection. Sometimes the judge may go as far as awarding you temporary exclusive occupancy of the marital home. In such cases, your spouse *Ejecting an* would receive an *order of ejectment;* in most situations he or *abusive* she would be given a reasonable amount of time to leave the *spouse* premises. The court also determines the duration of the order of protection, which is usually limited by law to one year.

Many areas have an Abused Spouse Hotline, which can be of invaluable assistance. Very often, your telephone operator *Abused* can provide you with the number, and we suggest that you *Spouse Hot-* contact the organization. Not only can its staff provide impor- *line* tant psychological counseling and information about temporary shelters, but they are also up to date on the various court procedures available to you.

My husband has always had a terrible temper, but when I told him that I wanted a divorce, things really got out of hand. I have nowhere to go, and he refuses to leave the home. Is there any way I can protect myself from further outbursts?

If by "further outbursts" you merely mean temper tantrums, then probably not. The idea of an order of protection is not necessarily to protect your eardrums. There is, however, no general rule when it comes to this type of court protection. In each case the facts are different, and so are the judge's atti- *Temper tan-* tudes. If you can readily show that these outbursts have a de- *trums* bilitating effect, such as making it impossible for you to sleep or to concentrate on your work, there is a chance that you will obtain an order of protection. The only thing you have to lose by trying is time. No one says that you have to wait until you get a black eye before you can come to court.

Are threats enough?

Sometimes they can be, and an order of protection may be granted because the threats not only pose a danger to you but inhibit the exercise of your rights.

Several years ago, Linda came to our office to consult us about starting a divorce action. She certainly had grounds, and

Threats of physical harm

there was no question in her mind that she wanted out of the marriage. However, she was extremely distraught and nervous about proceeding. She told us that her husband had threatened to "beat the daylights out of her" if he was ever served with divorce papers. Although he had never layed a hand upon her, she explained that he had been an amateur boxer. Linda's financial circumstances did not allow her to move away from the home, which would have been one way to ensure her safety.

Protecting your right to seek dissolution of marriage

Therefore, a decision was made to accompany Linda to the Family Court to seek a temporary order of protection. It was explained to the judge that our client had reason to believe the sincerity of her husband's threat, that she was afraid to commence a divorce and that these threats interfered with her right to seek dissolution of the marriage in court. The judge agreed, and she granted Linda a temporary order of protection.

Once Linda's husband received a copy of the temporary order of protection, he went to his lawyer. His attorney advised him that he would have to be especially careful at this point; any abuse of his wife could have very serious repercussions. A permanent order of protection was made by the court on consent of the parties and their attorneys. The divorce action was started, and while it was bitterly contested, not one fist was raised in anger.

He told me last night that a wife is a husband's property, and that he could do with me whatever he wanted. When I refused to have intercourse with him, he forced himself upon me and physically assaulted me. I feel no better than a rape victim, and I want to know if I can file criminal rape charges against my husband.

Most states forbid rape charges

Probably not. Most states prohibit a wife from charging her husband with rape. Of course, your husband's conduct may sustain a criminal assault charge and should certainly entitle you to an order of protection.

There has been considerable debate lately over amending the criminal laws to encompass interspousal rape. However, society does not yet seem ready to interfere in the marital bedroom. One of the crucial elements in a rape case is the lack of the victim's consent. This becomes troublesome in a marital context where consent is deemed implicit in the relationship. Some states, such as New York, will go so far as to prosecute a husband for rape if the act occurred while the parties were sep-

Consent is a crucial element

arated, presumably because the implied consent no longer exists under those circumstances.

Some exceptions exist. California, for the most part, represents the leading edge of the law. Thus it is not surprising that *California is* in 1979 it added to its penal code section 262, entitled "Rape of *an exception* Spouse." It defines interspousal rape as "an act of sexual intercourse accomplished against the will of the spouse by means of force or fear of immediate and unlawful bodily injury." A conviction can result in imprisonment for a maximum of eight years. There is, however, one important proviso. The spouse must report the violation within thirty days to the local district attorney. (Notice we say "spouse"; we believe the statute can be read so as to permit a charge by the husband!) While this law may be a sign of things to come, many experts believe that it will take years for attitudes and laws to change in other jurisdictions.

Since I moved out of the house, I have developed a friendship at work—nothing romantic, but I enjoy his company. The other night, we ran into my husband while dining at the local restaurant. I was shocked to hear my estranged spouse threaten my friend with a "fat lip" if he ever saw the two of us together again. Is there any process by which my friend can be protected from the possibility of physical harm?

Only he can protect himself. Ordinarily, orders of protection *Reduce* extend to the spouse and to his or her immediate family and *chance en-* household members. There is nothing that you can do except *counters* reduce the chance of encounters.

There is nothing stopping your friend, however, from seeking whatever other protection may be available. Certainly if *Press criminal* your husband assaults him, your friend can make a complaint *charges* to the police. Ironically, the police would be more responsive to such a dispute, because it is not a marital one. In such a case your husband would be arrested and possibly prosecuted on a criminal charge.

My husband's loathsome behavior has already forced me from the home. I am temporarily residing with my sister at her apart- *Protection ex-* *ment. Last night, he came around and threatened my sister and* *tended to* *me. Can I obtain an order of protection and will my sister be* *household* *protected as well?* *members*

Yes. You needn't be living under the same roof with your spouse to qualify for an order. Threatening conduct remains threatening conduct no matter where it occurs. Thus, you may apply for the order of protection, and so long as you can demonstrate that your husband poses a real and present danger to your well-being, you will get it.

As far as your sister is concerned, most states provide that orders of protection will apply to family and household members upon a showing of good cause. Similar proof will be required concerning the effect of your husband's conduct on your sister's safety and well-being as would be required from you.

I've been reading all this about orders of protection, but can I get one against my wife?

Gender-neutral

Yes. Orders of protection know no gender. You may be in a situation where your physical or mental well-being is endangered. We once had a client whose wife had a habit of sneaking up behind him and attempting to strangle him with a dishrag, and he had no trouble obtaining an order of protection.

Am I really protected by such an order?

No magic shield

An order of protection is not, alas, a magic shield. If your spouse is intent on causing you harm—and this can happen in a situation where emotions run high—no piece of paper is going to stop a physical assault. However, the benefit of the order is not illusory. First, it is symbolic of the state's intervention and the possible reach of the law. Second, should a dispute

Best bet

break out and the police be called in, they will not turn their heads and tell you to work things out for yourselves. If you are able to show an officer an order of protection, it is very likely that your spouse will spend the night in the pokey. Criminal charges may then be brought against him, which is something that may make an enraged spouse think twice before laying his or her hand on you. In California, for example, a willful violation of an order of protection is a misdemeanor punishable by a maximum $500 fine or six months' imprisonment, or both;

Landing in jail

moreover, inflicting on a spouse bodily injury which results in "a traumatic condition" is a felony punishable by up to four years in the state prison. If you are in a dangerous situation, there is really no true protection except avoiding all contact with your spouse. However, for many this is not a realistic solution, and they can only turn to the imperfect ones, such as an order of protection.

What does an order of protection say?

The language of an order of protection varies from state to state. However, the following is typical of the heart of any order of protection:

> NOW THEREFORE, upon all the papers and proceedings had herein, it is
>
> ORDERED that the respondent/husband shall observe the following conditions of behavior:
>
> 1. Abstain from offensive conduct against the petitioner/wife;
>
> 2. Abstain from offensive conduct against the children;
>
> 3. Refrain from acts of commission or omission that tend to make the home not a proper place for the family or any household member;
>
> 4. Cease all other forms of harassment, abuse, menacing and threatening conduct toward the petitioner/wife;
>
> 5. Refrain from any acts or threats of physical violence upon the petitioner/wife or any other member of the household;
>
> AND IT IS FURTHER
>
> ORDERED that the directions herein shall be and remain in force until the further order of this court; and it is further
>
> ORDERED that the clerk of the court file a copy of this Order, and any amendments thereto, with the appropriate police agency having jurisdiction in this matter.

The order of protection may also include warnings in large boldface type, such as this one that is required in Texas:

A VIOLATION OF THIS ORDER BY COMMISSION OF FAMILY VIOLENCE MAY BE A CRIMINAL OFFENSE PUNISHABLE BY A FINE OF AS MUCH AS $2,000 OR BY CONFINEMENT IN JAIL FOR AS LONG AS ONE YEAR, OR BOTH.

My wife's outbursts are becoming more frequent and increasingly vocal. I'm not really afraid of her threats, but her yelling and screaming are beginning to disturb the other tenants. I am convinced that the landlord may ask us to leave. What can I do to protect myself?

You may be able to obtain an order of protection in such a case if you can convince the court that the situation poses a real and actual threat to the marital home. Obviously, if there is a real possibility of being evicted because of your wife's conduct, a court will issue an order directing her to cease such outbursts. If she refuses, she may find herself held in contempt of court. Moreover, you may be able to call the police and have her removed from the premises on the strength of the order of protection, something that you could never do without one.

Chapter Two
WHAT ABOUT
THE CHILDREN?

Children are all too often caught in the middle of their parents' divorce. Many times they become the unwitting pawns of the contest, virtually held hostage to disputes over financial support and visitation. Some parents, caught in the orbit of their own fears, motives and vindictiveness, lose sight of their children's welfare as they try to score points—both legal and psychological—at their children's expense. Any divorce carries with it tremendous potential for lasting harm, and parents must be on vigilant guard to ensure that they do their utmost to shield the children from the problems of a broken marriage. These problems are magnified whenever custody becomes an unresolved issue. Suddenly the children are inexorably swept into the very center of the controversy and become active participants in the divorce process.

Much has been written about the psychological impact of divorce on children. While we are not qualified to offer any professional advice in this area, which is nonetheless as important as the legal side of the coin, our own experience and discussions with psychiatrists specializing in the field reveal a virtual consensus that the best course is for both parents to be open and candid about the divorce from the outset. They suggest that parents take the initiative and discuss the divorce and its anticipated consequences in concrete and honest terms, making sure that the children realize that they will continue to have access to the non-custodial parent and that they did not have anything to do with the underlying reasons for the breakup itself. As practicing attorneys, we can only add that parents must avoid needlessly involving their children in the legal complexities of the case. You don't need a lawyer to point out the insidious danger of telling the kids, "Your old man is a cheap bum; he's offered only fifty dollars a week for child support."

There is, of course, the all-important legal side involving children, the area upon which this chapter focuses. Having an idea of how the system affects your rights, obligations and interests as well as the parent-child relationship is perhaps the best safeguard against involving your son or daughter in a disastrous legal entanglement. The more knowledge you have, the better the chance that you and your spouse may come to an amicable understanding that saves everyone from the aftershock of litigation. This is not to say that there exists a perfect solution for every crisis involving children. Far from it. But how you approach these difficulties may make all the difference between creating an environment where the parent–child relationship is nurtured and one in which you watch helplessly on the shore as your children are cast adrift on the turbulent seas of marital discord.

CHILD'S DAY IN COURT

Will my child have to testify in court?

Only in custody cases

Maybe. Children do not ordinarily testify in divorce trials unless custody is at issue. Even then age is an important consideration.

Before a child testifies, the court inquires whether he or she is old enough to understand the nature of an oath. The judge tries to get a feeling of the child's maturity. Each have different

Age important factor

standards, so there is no absolute rule as to how old the child has to be before he or she is permitted to testify. Even if the child is too young or immature, the judge will often have an *in camera* conference with him or her. *In camera* literally means "in room"; the session usually takes place in the judge's chambers, away from the parents, lawyers and witnesses. No one is present except the child and the judge, and sometimes a court

Private hearing

reporter. If the session is recorded, the child's statements are as a rule sealed and available to no one except the judge. The purpose of the hearing is to permit the child to talk freely about his or her relationship with the mother and father. The child's preference to live with one or the other parent will also be explored. As will be seen, this is a factor that the judge takes into account in determining custody, but it is only one of many.

If you anticipate that there will be a custody dispute, you can explain to your child that the judge may want to hear his or her own story. Then have the strength to drop it. You know more than anyone else how easily manipulated children are, and this is a time when parents are often tempted to begin to coach the child. Instead, just tell your child that he or she has nothing to be afraid of, and that the judge and the lawyers are all working together to find a solution that will be best for everyone. You should also explain to the child that sometimes the court may appoint a lawyer, called a *guardian ad litem,* to represent the child's interests. This lawyer acts as an objective fact-finder and "buffer" between his or her more adversarial counterparts representing the parents. In any custody dispute, the child's best interests are paramount, and the law guardian attempts to make sure that this point is never lost. *Appointment of law guardian for child*

In one recent New York case a thirteen-year-old child demanded that she be represented by a lawyer, and the court immediately appointed a legal guardian. She felt that she had her own story to tell and that it would be impossible if she was forced to work through her parents' lawyers. Indeed, you may wish to explore the possibility with your own attorney, requesting that the court appoint a *guardian ad litem* for the children.

Finally, courts today increasingly rely on family counseling services whenever custody becomes an issue. Therefore, you should explain to your child that he or she may be interviewed by a psychologist, family counselor or even a psychiatrist. These professionals then provide the judge with a written or oral report of their impressions and recommendations. Tell the child to be truthful with the interviewer and that there is no reason to feel that there is anything to hide. Explain that the counselor is there for only one purpose—to help the child and to assist the court in determining where the best place is for him or her to reside. *Court-ordered reports from counselors and psychiatrists*

If the court is forced to determine custody, will the judge ask my child whom she loves better?

No. Even if the issue of custody goes to trial and must be determined by a judge, the question of comparative "love" will never be raised. No judge will put your child in a position of having to answer that kind of question, and you can tell your daughter that.

However, you should know that a judge may ask your child whom she wants to live with. Preference is a factor in custody cases and will be considered before the court finally resolves *Child's pref-* who the custodial parent will be. However, such preference is *erence not de-* not determinative; just because Cindy is suddenly articulating *terminative* a keen desire to move in with her father does not necessarily mean that her argument will sway the judge. The younger the child, the less weight his or her preference will have.

The courts fully understand that a child can be easily manipulated by a bitter or even well-meaning parent and that the desires of children are often transient and may not reflect their own best interests.

One last bit of advice: if it seems that a custody battle is *Don't manip-* really shaping up, you must resist the impulse to curry favor *ulate* with your child. A judge will be on the lookout for any evidence of "wrongful influence," and any preference articulated by your child will be given even less weight than usual.

VISITATION AND CUSTODY

She calls me at work and informs me that I'll never see our kid again. Now what?

You must first decide whether your wife is serious. Often such threats are made in the heat of the moment. Psychological *Children as* warfare is common in divorces. Sadly, children are used as *hostages* hostages. If you believe that your wife is going to make good on her word, you must act quickly. This is the time to contact your attorney, or to obtain one, if you haven't already done so.

Assuming for the moment that you both have lawyers, your attorney will contact your wife's. This is one of those instances *Contact law-* where attorneys work together. Your wife's lawyer will as-*yer* suredly explain to her the grave consequences of her unilateral actions. More times than not, this is enough. If your wife has not yet retained an attorney, your lawyer will probably write or telephone her directly, advising her that if she does not change her position a court proceeding will be brought immediately to ensure your rights to see the child.

If your wife refuses to be persuaded either by her attorney or *Equal custo-* yours, there is no alternative but to commence a court pro-*dial rights* ceeding. Before anyone goes to court, both parents have an equal right to custody and visitation. The traditional legal view that presumed the mother to be a more suitable custodial parent has been abolished in almost every state. If you have moved out, you do not automatically lose this right; as a parent you are permitted access to your child. Therefore, you can initiate a proceeding to enforce your visitation rights. Procedures *Possibility of* differ from state to state, but the result is the same—a court *contempt* order. If your wife refuses to obey this order, she can be held in contempt, and in some instances even lose her custodial rights.

Is there any way a judge can deny me a visitation order?

Yes. Your right to see your child is not absolute. Sammy steadfastly refused, for six months to pay his wife any money for her support and the child's. In his version of psychological warfare, he believed that if he could bring her to her knees financially, she would become desperate and accept any amount of support he dictated. Yet he would be at the door every Sun- *Visitation is* day morning waiting to take his son out for the day. He ig- *conditional* nored Betty's pleas for some help. One Sunday she refused to answer the doorbell.

Sammy went running to his lawyer, screaming, "I'm being denied my visitation. She won't let me see the kid."

Without exploring the underlying facts further, Sammy's lawyer drew up legal papers, which were served on Betty the next day. A court date was set. Betty could not afford an attorney, but as it turned out she really did not need one. Once she told the judge that she had not received a dime from Sammy for the last six months, the judge turned a steely eye toward him and ruled that his right to visit their son was dependent on his paying child support. The court set the figure and told Sammy that unless he paid this sum each week, his wife did not have to let him see the boy.

The judge's decision was based upon a legal concept called *linkage.* The modern trend is to link the right of visitation to *Linkage* child support; you cannot have one without the other.

What should I do about my wife not letting me talk to my daughter on the phone?

Although your wife's conduct cannot be condoned, this is really one of those gray areas where no easy answer can be supplied. Technically speaking, your right to visitation does *Law not ex-* not extend to telephoning the child. Courts are loath to get in- *plicit* volved in such minutiae. For example, your wife can claim that the child was in the bathtub, sleeping or otherwise indisposed, and who is to say that she is not telling the truth?

This does not mean that you are entirely powerless. Continue to maintain contact with your child in innovative ways. *Make innovative contact* Write letters, send her a telegram, wire flowers. Maybe you can see her in the afternoon at school during recess or lunch break. Make good use of your visitation time. Be sure to tell her that you have tried calling her but that you are always told that she is unavailable. Tell her you'll telephone every Wednesday evening at seven; then make sure that you do.

The second thing to do is talk to your wife. Explain that this little game helps no one and hurts your daughter. Explore the reasons for her actions. Does she have legitimate cause for *Discuss with spouse* such bitterness? Have you been living up to your end of the bargain? Once these issues are brought to the forefront, you can begin focusing on their resolution. No conflict between you and your wife will ever be solved by using your daughter as a pawn.

Another step that you can take is to inform your lawyer of the situation. Once again, he or she can work with your wife's *Inform lawyer* attorney in reaching an immediate accord. Sometimes a trusted friend or relative can be used as an intermediary who will stress the needs of the child as the paramount consideration.

I can no longer stay with my wife, but I can't possibly take the children with me now. Does that mean I will lose custody forever?

Not necessarily. Once the divorce papers are served and *Freezing custody issue* custody is presented as an issue, your rights will be preserved. This assumes that you act immediately in retaining an attorney and in beginning the divorce action. If you let three years go by after you have moved out and then seek to obtain custody, your chances are next to dismal. One of the major factors that a court will weigh in determining custody is *continuity,* i.e., the length of time the child has been living with one parent. Since your wife will have by then established a custodial relationship of several years, a court will presume that it is in your children's best interests to remain with her. Uprooting the children *Continuity is important factor* and making it necessary for them to change schools and friends are frowned upon, and will only be done in the most unusual circumstances. Remember, all custodial decisions turn upon "the best interests of the child"—not what is best for you or best for your wife.

But can't my divorce take a few years?

This does not matter. The time that is important is when you make your claim for custody. If you were the one that left the home, it might not have been feasible to take your child with you. Judges understand the practical considerations inherent in any divorce, so the fact that you've left your child behind usually will not adversely affect your chances of obtaining custody. Nevertheless, you will have to be sure to maintain close contact during the interim so that there will be no doubt as to the sincerity of your request. This does not only mean spending time with your child but also includes seeing your child's teachers, paying child support according to your means and in general maintaining an unquestionable parental interest in your child's welfare and upbringing.

Leaving your child behind

Maintaining meaningful contact

My friend claims that if I do not give up my job as a cocktail waitress I will lose custody of my children. Is that right?

Probably not. Your job does not necessarily imply bad morals or parental unfitness, major issues in any custody dispute.

All custody determinations are based upon "the best interests of the children." If your husband demands custody, the court will weigh such factors as parental fitness and conduct, financial ability to provide a home, the environment of the home, the emotional and economic stability of the parents and, in general, the parents' history with the children. As long as your job does not have a negative effect in any of these areas, you have nothing to worry about. However, while it is not the mere fact that you are a cocktail waitress upon which a custody determination will turn, some aspects of your job may lead a court to conclude that the children would be better off with their father.

Many factors considered

For example, your hours are important. If you are working during the day when the children are in school, there is no problem. Quite different is the case where you are working from the evening until the early hours of the morning and leaving your children with friends or babysitters. Your ability to properly supervise the children is certainly a factor that will be scrutinized by the judge. You cannot be an absent parent and expect to prevail in a custody dispute.

Job hours important

The atmosphere and nature of your workplace can also play a role. If your club or restaurant is frequented by shady charac-

Absent parents: beware

ters, drugs are used on the premises, several violent incidents have occurred or anything of the sort, a judge may infer from such facts doubts about your moral character, even though there is no proof that you were ever involved in anything other than serving drinks. The judge may openly question the character of a mother who would work in a place like that, and this *You are best* will undoubtedly influence his or her decision. You are the best *judge* judge. If you believe that the hours or company you keep will have an adverse effect in your case, you had best start reading the classified ads.

If your hours are reasonable and your place of employment does not have a bad reputation, there is no reason why a judge should deem you unfit as a parent merely because you are a cocktail waitress. Rather, the court will focus on those factors that relate to your ability to be a proper parent to your children. It is what you do with your children and not what you do for a living that counts.

I understand what you're saying, but in my town the only job I could get to support my kids was working late nights at the Kitty Kat Lounge—certainly a place I would never take my kids to. If I want to keep custody, will I be forced to quit?

Not necessarily. There are really no absolute rules when *Exceptional* it comes to divorce and custody disputes. Ordinarily, we *circumstances* would say that you would be taking an unnecessary chance by staying with your job, but sometimes exceptional circumstances, such as those in your case, can actually work to your advantage.

The fact that you have shown an initiative to provide the best support for the family reflects positively upon your sincerity and devotion to them. This is especially true if your husband provides inadequate or no financial support. You will have to be sure, however, that these facts come out in court, making clear that you had no alternative. Show the court that the arrangements for your children's supervision are more than satisfactory. Have the babysitter testify. She should be someone of maturity and responsibility, who will be able to state that you can always be reached by telephone in the event of an emergency. Your testimony should include your activities during your free time with the children, such as supervising home- *Arrange su-* work, visiting teachers, family outings and the like. It is not the *pervision* quantity of time you spend with your children, or even for that

matter the time of day; rather, it is the quality of that time—
what you do with it.

*I left my family seven months ago during which time I have not
spent much time with my daughter, but now that I'm settled in my
new apartment, I would like to have her live with me. My husband says that if I want custody, I will have to fight for it. Should
I do something now or wait until we go to trial?*

When you say "*I* would like to have her live with me," we
pause before we answer your question. Too frequently parents *Evaluate your*
consider what *they* want without paying any attention to what *motives*
are the best circumstances for the child. Before you do anything, explore the reasons why you feel you should have custody of your daughter. Are you lonely? Is there ego involved?
Is this a popularity contest? Has your child stated a preference?
After you have honestly answered these questions and con-
cluded that your reasons are valid, you are in a position to
weigh the various factors and problems confronting you.

First, the longer the wait the more difficult your position will
be. Custodial *continuity* is an important factor; the longer a *Retain lawyer*
child lives with one parent, the better that parent's chances are *immediately*
to retain custody. Thus, if no request has yet been made on
your behalf for custody, it is vital that you see an attorney immediately so that one can be made.

Having made custody an issue in your divorce (the procedure for this varies from state to state), the next important
thing for you to do is to initiate and maintain close parental
contact with your daughter, involving yourself as much as pos- *Regular and*
sible in all of her activities. Without a regular course of such *consistent*
conduct, a demand for custody is a meaningless gesture. Do *course of con-*
not, however, go overboard. Your actions should not be the *tact*
type that can be construed as an attempt to bribe or manipu-
late your child.

Because a divorce case often takes months or even years to
get to trial, your lawyer may advise you to make a request for
temporary custody. This will usually entail a pretrial hearing, *Possibility of*
replete with testimony of several witnesses and even psycho- *temporary*
logical reports. The court's determination, however, is not *ruling*
final. It is only a temporary stopgap that awaits fuller disclosure and final resolution at the trial. Many judges are loath to
conduct pretrial custody hearings for several reasons. First,

custody proceedings, even preliminary ones, consume much of the court's time. Second, they require intense preparation by the attorneys, time that often could be better spent getting the divorce case ready for trial. Third, it is often ill-advised to make any change of custody until there is a full hearing on all the issues; until all the facts are in, the status quo is rarely upset. Consequently, your chances of obtaining temporary custody may be remote unless you can demonstrate to the court several critical factors.

Preserving the status quo

If your child's environment is truly threatening, and your husband is indeed an unfit parent, you may be able to obtain temporary custody of your daughter. However, the degree of his unfitness and the threats to your child's welfare have to be clear and convincing before a judge will order a hearing. The judge will first want to examine closely your statements made in the sworn affidavits that your lawyer will submit to the court. Your husband will, of course, have an opportunity to reply to these allegations in his own sworn statement.

Exchanging affidavits

Also, do not lose sight of the fact that since there is no court order relating to custody at this early stage of your divorce, you both have legal custody of your child. It so happens that at the present time your husband has physical custody, but as a legal custodian of the child you are still permitted to take an active part in making all those decisions that affect the child, for example, schooling and health care. Nevertheless, you must respect the status quo—a situation that you yourself helped create. The fact remains that your daughter has resided with your husband for seven months. It would be wrong for you to snatch the child away from him. Not only would this demonstrate your irresponsibility and instability, but it is one of the most psychologically harmful things that you can do to your daughter. You can be sure that these actions would lead to your husband going into court for an order returning the child to him. Your action would do nothing but help destroy your chances of obtaining permanent custody of your daughter. Therefore, unless you are entitled to a preliminary hearing, you must bide your time and make the best use of it.

Right of consultation in child-rearing decisions

Childsnatching evidences irresponsibility and instability

My wife keeps telling me that my kids don't want to see me or talk to me. How can I find out if she's telling the truth?

Children may offer solution

Ask the kids. It is not uncommon in these emotionally trying times to lose sight of the most obvious solutions. If your children are old enough to make a decision not to speak to you, they are certainly old enough to openly discuss their reasons. There may be some underlying animosity toward you for having left home, or fears of what is to become of them. Explore these anxieties with them, always leaving open an avenue of communication.

COLLATERAL ISSUES

Since my husband moved out of our home, he insists upon seeing our sons every weekend. My friend says that the way to get back at him is for me to refuse to allow him to see the kids. At least it will bring him to his knees, says my neighbor. Good advice?

The worst advice. So long as there is no court order pertaining to custody, the law is clear that both you and your husband have equal legal custody of the children. Your husband did not relinquish this by moving out of the home. He is entitled to liberal access to his sons, a right which our courts vigorously protect. Of course, reasonableness controls. He should not just drop in to visit without first calling, which could be potentially disruptive and interfere with the family's plans. Nor can he insist upon spending every hour of each weekend with your sons; certainly you are entitled to some of this free time as well. *Visitation rights vigorously protected*

Reasonableness as controlling factor

As attorneys, we are always distressed when a client indicates a desire to "get back" at a spouse through the children. Nothing hurts the children or causes more unnecessary trouble than such an attitude. It can even ruin the client's case, for a judge is entitled to draw the most negative inferences from such conduct. We can understand that you may be bitter and angry at your husband. Perhaps the breakup was entirely his fault, at least the way you see it, but your children should not be the ones to march in the front lines of your battle. If you continue to harbor these feelings, the best advice that anyone can give you is to seek professional counseling. *Control bitterness*

Our home is in bedlam. My husband refuses to leave, and we do nothing but argue. I am afraid for the children and have made tentative plans to send them out of state to stay with my parents until things calm down. Am I doing the right thing or will my plan backfire on me? *Willful and malicious interference*

This would be in most cases an ill-advised course of conduct.

Your sending the children away can only be viewed as a malicious, willful effort to frustrate your husband's custodial rights. Moreover, your children can suffer psychological harm. They may believe that they are the cause of the marital problem and that is why they are being sent away. On the most practical level, your plan will interfere with their schooling and friendships. Exposing your child to arguments really causes them little harm. Actually, this experience may go a long way in eventually making them understand the reasons for the divorce. *Don't shield children from arguments* Shield them from the arguments and they will have a harder time coming to terms with the family breakup.

What if our arguments are becoming violent? My husband has slapped me several times. Am I entitled to move the children under these circumstances?

Order of protection is possible solution Even then, your plan is wrong. Your solution should be to obtain a temporary order of protection, which was discussed in the preceding chapter. This order can also grant you exclusive temporary occupancy of the marital home. Your husband will be forced to leave, but you and your children will remain in the regular family environment. The disruption to their lives will be minimized.

Just about the only circumstance that will justify sending the children from the home would be if your husband's behavior puts the children in real physical danger. For example, if your husband is an alcoholic who becomes violent, he may not be aware of his actions. Then you should get the children out of the house until the wheels of justice have begun turning. However, look for a closer haven for your children, preferably one in the same neighborhood or town. Moving them out of the state is too unsettling, and it carries unnecessary negative connotations.

I've been reading so much about childsnatching recently. What kind of protection do I have in this regard?

Government's hands-off approach To be honest, not much. Historically, family controversies have always been considered the state's sole domain. The federal government has traditionally adopted a hands-off approach, so when a child is taken across state lines without authorization, bureaucratic paralysis sets in. The local police, prosecutors, state troopers and other executive branches of government are averse to interfere in matrimonial matters, adding to the helplessness and confusion that pervades the issue of parental kidnapping. However, inroads have been made, and a spouse living through the hell of a childsnatching may be able to take advantage of legal procedures that have recently been enacted on a nationwide scale.

We are referring to the Federal Parental Kidnapping Prevention Act of 1980. For you to obtain the benefit of this law, *Federal kid-* the wrongful taking and the later concealment and refusal to *napping law* return the child must be a *felony* under your state's law. Custo- *recently en-* dial interference—childsnatching—is a crime in most states; *acted* however, it is classified only as a mere misdemeanor in quite a few. If custodial interference or child abduction is a felonious act in your state, then the FBI may be called in to assist in locating the child, and the U.S. Attorney's Office may prosecute the guilty spouse. The problem, unfortunately, is that many states have not yet gotten around to making this reprehensible conduct a felony. As of the writing of this book, several states *Must be a fel-* have introduced the needed amendments to their penal laws, *ony* and it is anticipated that the trend will continue. Rather than providing a state-by-state listing that will probably be outdated by the time that you read this, we suggest that you simply inquire at the local prosecutor's office for the necessary information.

In addition to the federal law, forty-five states have adopted the Uniform Child Custody Jurisdiction Act (UCCJA). The *Most states* avowed purpose of the act is to avoid jurisdictional competi- *have adopted* tion and to promote cooperation with the courts of other states. *Uniform Act* To understand the importance of this legislation, you must first realize that in the old days—and by "old" we do not mean too many years ago—every state court was absolutely free to ignore a sister state's prior custody order. Thus, if James lost his custody battle in Connecticut he could surreptitiously take his child to Texas and start all over again. You guessed it: this type of procedural loophole encouraged childsnatching, as losing spouses got another chance to plead their cases in the state of *Forum shop-* their choice. Lawyers call this "forum shopping," and it is not *ping dis-* looked upon with favor. *couraged*

With the enactment of the UCCJA, judges now must carefully scrutinize another state's custody decision before relitigating the matter. The original decision will be upheld unless the spouse seeking the modification can demonstrate several specific and highly technical grounds. At the very least, no *Upholding the* modification will be allowed if it appears that the parent re- *prior order* questing the change in custody is merely in the state for that reason and has had no other significant contact, such as a prior six-month residence.

Act is only some help; not perfect

The act is not a perfect solution. The most obvious flaw is that it only applies to situations where a previous custody order has already been rendered. Unfortunately, the law is of little help when the snatching occurs before a divorce case has been commenced. We would be totally remiss if we did not stop to note that Mr. Arnold I. Miller, head of Children's Rights, Inc., of Washington, D.C., estimates that perhaps seven out of ten parents who are subjected to the cruelty of childnapping never see the child again.

May use locator services

In addition to legal mechanisms, childsnatching victims may also avail themselves of federal and state parent locator services. The organizations are geared toward tracing the missing spouse and child. If they are found, the victim may then travel to that particular state and commence an immediate action for return of custody. Sadly, these services are far too expensive for parents of modest means.

Don't just sit there

The specter of parental kidnapping continues to haunt the matrimonial field. About the only advice we can give is to emphasize that you must act immediately if you suspect that you have become a victim. Call a lawyer. Contact the police. Do not sit around feeling sorry for yourself. Every second wasted puts another mile between you and your child.

Chapter Three
MONEY AND SUPPORT

The unexpected end of the marriage can often result in severe financial emergencies or hardships. Often the financial needs of a dependent spouse are ignored, either unconsciously or vindictively, by the other spouse. With little savings and no outside source of income, a mortgage payment due and the local utility threatening to turn off the juice, something must be done. The good news is that every state has procedures whereby a person may commence a proceeding against his or her spouse for support; the bad news is that the process in some states is a time-consuming proposition.

The first and smartest step is to discuss your real needs with your spouse in an effort to reach an informal arrangement. If this fails, you have little choice but to start a support proceeding.

SUPPORT OBLIGATIONS

Before starting any discussions, you should have an idea of your respective support obligations and rights. Support is not charity; it is required by law. The extent of this responsibility depends upon the circumstances of your case, encompassing everything from the length of your marriage to your pre-separation standard of living. Of course, the ability to pay plays an important role as well.

My wife and I are having an argument. Although we both believe that a divorce is the only solution to our marital difficulties, she says that she is going to ask the court to give her alimony. I say that she's got no right to financial support because she is working. Just what are my legal rights in this regard?

Economic partnership

The modern trend is to view marriage as an economic partnership. Proceeding from this premise, judges attempt to achieve a fair division of the parties' property which can sometimes diminish, if not eliminate, the need for alimony or maintenance. For example, if both spouses have a home, joint bank accounts, some stock and a couple of automobiles, the division of these assets may suffice to give each a new lease on life, especially in a situation like yours where both are employed.

Husband's traditional duty to support wife

To understand alimony, you must look at it from its historical perspective. The law is only a reflection of societal mores. Traditionally, it was a man's duty to support his wife. Even up until very recently, a woman was very often entirely dependent upon her husband's income. Two-income families had not evolved to any great degree. When the parties divorced, the husband could not escape his obligations to support his wife. Meanwhile, the husband retained most of the assets. This reflected the old, now almost totally discarded view that because property was usually in the man's name, it was solely his.

Modern view

Times have changed. Women work and have their own careers, assets, property and investments. They are no longer as dependent upon their husbands' income. The wife's economic independence has at the same time tended to liberate the husband from a duty to support her for the rest of her life or until she remarries. Since marital property will now be divided in most states between the parties in an equitable or equal fashion, there is rarely reason to compel permanent monthly alimony. In fact, in some states a spouse will receive alimony only if there exists an incapacitation which inhibits employment; for example, a serious illness or the necessity of assuming a supervisory role as chief caretaker for several infant children.

Duration of alimony or maintenance

This is not to say that wives no longer are awarded alimony or *maintenance,* as it is now called in most states. However, the trend is to shorten the duration of such payments and to rely more heavily on the division of marital assets and property. Alimony or maintenance is viewed as rehabilitative, that is, continuing only for as long as the wife's situation requires dependence on the husband's income. The wife's health, age and education, as well as the ages of the children, all play a determining role in fixing this period. For example, the children may be too young to allow the wife to immediately re-enter the job market, or perhaps the wife will first have to finish her college education for a degree in marketing. However, there still may be some situations in which the wife will be awarded permanent alimony. For example, a sixty-year-old woman who was married for forty years and has raised a family, never having worked in the interim, would be certain to obtain permanent alimony, unless her share of the couple's assets was so great as to ensure her sufficient income for the rest of her life. *Permanent alimony*

There are many factors that determine your wife's eligibility for alimony. The fact that she is employed is one, but there are many others.

What about child support? The kids will be staying with her. Again, she insists that I foot the bill.

Child support is today considered a *mutual* obligation, as opposed to the historic legal concept that it is entirely the husband's obligation. Both you and your wife, therefore, are responsible for the expenses of raising and educating the children. *Mutual obligation*

The extent of your individual responsibility will generally be in rough proportion to your income. However, in our experience, the non-custodial parent usually winds up paying more than a pro-rata share, because the other parent will be contributing more in the way of household services to the children, such as feeding them and washing their clothes. *Obligation proportional to your respective incomes*

Child support is usually fixed to provide satisfactory financial assistance to the custodial parent for the usual and reasonable expenses of child rearing. Sometimes the payments take into account anticipated medical and dental expenses, while at other times a specific provision is made that the non-custodial spouse pay all or part of such bills or maintain major medical coverage. There is also a recognizable trend of courts in certain instances to include the costs of the children's college educations as an element of the support obligation. *Ordinary and reasonable child-rearing expenses*

My wife moved out a few months ago, leaving me with our ten-month-old son. Between the cost of babysitters and everything, I can no longer afford to pay the mortgage from just my salary. Should my wife be contributing to this expense?

Assuming your wife is employed, she should be paying a share of the household expenses until a determination can be *Paying just share of household expenses* made as to what will be done with the house and other marital property. Of course, having moved out, she has her own separate expenses, e.g., rent, but this does not extinguish her financial responsibilities to her family and third parties such as the bank that holds the mortgage. It certainly behooves her to help with the mortgage payments so that her ownership interest in the home is protected.

I heard that a husband is responsible for paying his wife's bills. I honestly need to replace my winter coat. The store is willing to extend the credit. Can my husband be held responsible to pay for the coat?

Necessaries doctrine

Your husband can be held responsible if you live in one of those states that recognize the so-called *necessaries doctrine.* Most states still do in some form or another.

The necessaries doctrine holds that a husband is primarily responsible for necessities furnished to the wife by third persons who rely on the husband's income in giving credit to the wife; for example, the grocer who has been allowing you to charge your purchases for years, knowing that your husband comes in once a month to pay the bill. What falls under the category of necessaries depends on your particular standard of living, but certainly reasonable expenses for health care, food, clothing and shelter qualify. If your husband refuses to supply you with such necessaries, you may obligate him to foot the bill; the doctrine requires him to pay third persons directly for the goods or services that were provided to you. Some states have enacted legislation that says that both the husband and wife remain equally liable to third persons for necessaries, but this would still not disturb your right to seek reimbursement from your husband at a later date in the event that the entire bill was collected from you.

Modified by legislation in some states

Doctrine is beginning to erode

We believe that the necessaries doctrine is beginning to erode, and that it will eventually go the way of other anachronistic concepts such as permanent alimony. The husband is no longer automatically viewed as the main breadwinner. The necessaries doctrine implies that a wife is completely dependent on her husband, and this may not be entirely true in your case.

Nevertheless, if you need the coat but cannot afford to spend your money on it, charge it and worry about the consequences later. Just make sure that your purchase is reasonable. Forget the mink. A credit card or charge account is not a device that you should use to vent your feelings or engage in needless psychological warfare.

OPEN DISCUSSIONS

Do not be ashamed of your financial predicament. You should make every effort to contact your spouse to discuss your needs and those of the family. Pride or anger should not get in the way. Neither should panic. Therefore, you owe it to yourself and your family to test the waters and raise the subject of temporary support with your mate. Hopefully, an accord can be reached until the divorce is finalized. This may seem difficult, but it is much easier than trekking down to court and describing your needs to the judge.

My friends tell me not to discuss anything specific with my wife before retaining my own lawyer. Why do you advise open and frank discussions?

Going through a divorce is difficult enough without exacerbating the conflict by taking intractable positions. You must make an effort to distinguish between the two concurrent levels inherent in any divorce. First, there is the emotional side, the pain of the breakup and the anxiety about the future. Second, there are the practical considerations, such as support, child custody and property divisions. Confusing the two, or treating them the same way, will only make your divorce more difficult. Such an approach will create or intensify problems in your interactions with your spouse and will translate into much greater legal fees, time expenditure and litigation complexities. Finally, if you cannot resolve your own problems, a judge will have to do it. As well-meaning as he or she may be, the result may appear arbitrary, pleasing nobody. *Two levels in every divorce*

Assuming you still communicate with your spouse, there is no reason why you both cannot discuss openly the dollars and cents of your separation. Avoid the recriminations and any attempts to analyze where the marriage went wrong. That can be the subject of another talk. Instead focus on the practicalities—the mortgage, the fuel bill, how much each can afford to contribute while still maintaining an independent existence. Discuss the living arrangements. Does it pay to keep the house or the apartment? Or would it make more sense to sell it and divide the proceeds? With an open and honest approach, you *Avoid recriminations*

Focus on practicalities

will be surprised to learn how much common ground exists. Get the easy decisions out of the way, and leave the more difficult ones for another time. There is nothing that says you have to do all of this in one sitting. Often a few days to reconsider your position will allow further necessary compromise.

Compromise is essential

You and your wife must begin these discussions realizing that neither of you will get everything. Compromise is essential; if you do not do it, the judge certainly will. So begin as soon as you can. Perhaps some issues will have to be resolved in court, but that is no reason to shy away from the hard decisions that you should make for yourselves.

Divorce ends marriage but not the relationship

There is another benefit to having open and frank discussions. You must realize that divorce does not end the relationship, it only ends the marriage. If you have children, you will still be parents. Even if there are no children, certain aspects of your divorce may require future contact. There may, for example, be ongoing maintenance payments or a decision to sell some joint property in a few years. Some women discover that they may have to wait until their husbands retire, which is sometimes fifteen or twenty years down the road, before they can get their share of the retirement pension. Since the chances are good that you will have an ongoing relationship, it is foolish to do anything to jeopardize it now. By being sensible and reasonable you not only can resolve many of the practical issues, but you receive the added bonus of laying a good foundation for the future relationship with your spouse. A spirit of cooperation developed now will hold you in good stead in the years to come.

But suppose I agree to something foolish?

Lawyer as "fail-safe" mechanism

By foolish we assume you mean something that will be against your interests. Remember, we are talking about informal arrangements. We surely do not suggest that you and your wife make any permanent decisions without first consulting a lawyer. There may indeed be certain parts of your arrangement that are either legally invalid, impossible to enforce or deeply prejudicial to you.

Client's interests vs. lawyer's ego

Once you and your wife have set the groundwork, then go to your respective lawyers, who will review your understandings and determine whether to put them into proper, legally binding form. A word of caution: unfortunately, we must point out that some attorneys superimpose their own values and judgments without considering the time and effort already devoted by the parties. They often confuse their client's interests with the needs of their own egos, and may attempt to supersede what has already been agreed upon in an effort to enhance their own reputation. We were told by a client about a lawyer with whom she first consulted, who, upon hearing that the parties had essentially reached their own agreement, said, "Forget what you've done. I don't even want to know about it. That's why you've come to me." She was turned off by this attitude and approach, being unwilling to imbue the lawyer with omniscience, and she decided to seek other counsel.

This is not to say that your attorney will not have valid reservations about your informal agreements. However, he or she *Laying the* should be able to explain to you exactly where you went wrong *groundwork* and how it may prove harmful.

Henry had agreed to give his wife sole ownership of the three-bedroom ranch. He thought that this was a good deal because his wife said she would not ask for any alimony. As it turned out, she makes almost as much money as he does, and his lawyer explained to him that her chances of obtaining court-ordered alimony were remote. Henry also agreed to pay for his children's college education. Although he was somewhat surprised to learn that the law did not require him to do so, he told his lawyer that he wanted to pay for their education anyway. However, his lawyer asked him what he meant by "paying for college." Did this include the cost of room and board, travel expenses, weekly allowances, food and books? Henry said he did not know, and that he would have to talk to his wife again; they had never thought to raise these questions themselves.

Here we can see the benefit of informal agreements and a responsive attorney keyed into a client's needs. The lawyer used his expertise to sharpen the focus, while the arrangement itself *Sharpen focus* provided the primary basis for an amicable settlement. Their divorce decree ultimately incorporated a formal written agreement pretty much along the lines of the parties' original understanding. Henry's wife would remain in the house with the children until they were old enough for college, after which time the home would be sold and the proceeds divided equally *Symbiotic re-* between the parties. Henry would pay for the children's college *lationship be-* tuition, and the parties would divide equally the other related *tween client* expenses. In this case, a symbiotic relationship had been per- *and lawyer* mitted to grow, both Henry and his lawyer assisting one another in defining and refining the important issues.

All right, you have sold me on the idea of attempting an informal arrangement, but how do I broach the subject to my husband? He has already said that he wants to leave everything to his attorney.

Broaching the subject

It is impossible for us to give you an ironclad rule on how to go about persuading your husband to participate in these discussions. You know him and his moods; we don't. However, we can give you some general guidelines that are useful in most situations.

Begin with generalities

Do not begin with the specifics, but instead have a general, almost philosophical discussion with your husband. Tell him that you believe that you and he are in the best position to make certain decisions, and try to show him the benefits of keeping those decisions "in the family." The way *not* to approach it is to give him a list of demands as if you were holding hostages.

Determine reasons for spouse's fears

Next, try to explore the reasons for your husband's attitude. Very often it is based upon unfounded fears that the divorce will be very expensive for him. He may be worried about paying too much alimony or being "held up" for his possessions or half of his business. You can tell him that you are only attempting to get what you need. Don't say "deserve," even though you may feel like using that word instead. Such an approach will inevitably sidetrack your discussion into accusations and regrets.

Finally, you may overcome your husband's initial hesitancy by telling him that you do not expect to get anything in writing; that you are only interested at this early juncture in considering some of his thinking, not his lawyer's. Explain that there will be plenty of opportunity for him to consult with his attorney, who along with yours will draw up any formal agreements.

I've been out of the house for about four months, and recently my wife and I have had some discussions, as you advised. The trouble is that I think she's artificially inflating her weekly expenses to get more money from me. Is there any way I can convince her to be more realistic?

Mandatory disclosure

Perhaps your wife does not realize that she will eventually have to disclose, under oath, all of her assets, earnings and expenses, either at the trial or in a sworn written statement that is filed with the court. Financial disclosure, what lawyers call "discovery," is necessary in every divorce action where there are financial issues involved. We will be discussing this separately in a later chapter.

Thus, you can explain to your wife that she will eventually have to disclose her real expenses. Very often she must verify *Verify expenses* them by producing receipts, bills and canceled checks. This insight should convince her to be more accurate in her computations. Moreover, you should have the opportunity to go over these figures with her and determine the reasonableness and necessity of any expense. This is in essence what a judge will do should your divorce proceed to trial.

The idea at this stage is to reach an informal agreement. You should say that you are willing to pay for certain expenses that are readily verifiable, such as rent, mortgage, taxes, food and utilities. Perhaps there is an outstanding medical bill that is *Some help* overdue. Your wife should realize that it is better to get some *now, maybe* economic assistance at this stage, and if there really is a need *more later* for more money, her attorney can assist her in obtaining more later. For now your goal is to reach an understanding and compromise with respect to most of the important expenses.

During these past four months, my wife has gotten a job. Shouldn't that be considered now?

Absolutely. The ideal solution is that you each contribute to living expenses in proportion to your income. Of course, no ar- *Dual support* rangement is perfect, and for your own reasons you may agree *obligations* to pay more or less than your share. This notion of dual financial responsibility is especially true for child support obligations, which are increasingly viewed today as a *mutual* obligation of both parents—a far cry from the days when a court would look solely to the father for any monetary contributions for the support of the children.

INFORMAL ARRANGEMENTS

Your goal is to reach a temporary mutual understanding that tides everyone over until the uncertainties are dispelled by the final divorce judgment. The more agreement, the less chance of litigation. The delivery of a divorce summons does not necessarily mean that all meaningful communication must cease. Most couples do not realize how much flexibility they have in fashioning their own relief—relief that may be tailored to the parties' individual situations and needs. Virtually every issue can be readily solved, at least temporarily, if the two spouses set their minds to it and do not permit the existence of the divorce action to cloud their judgment.

My wife is pushing me to pay her $125 a week during our trial separation. I fear that this informal arrangement may lock me into these weekly payments when we go to court. Are my fears well founded?

Voluntary payments not controlling

No. The voluntary payments to your wife will not be controlling; however, they may be indicative of your wife's needs and your ability to pay. This is just one element among many that the judge will consider before fixing alimony or maintenance.

Yes, but as it turns out I cannot really afford to keep paying her $125 every week. Yet you say that the judge will look at my payments as proof that I can afford it. Will this work to my disadvantage?

Future modification

Probably not. As we have already said, your attorney will be introducing other evidence of your wife's needs and your means. If you truly cannot afford these payments, your attorney will have an opportunity to demonstrate this by allowing you to testify as to your weekly expenses. As long as you can prove these expenses, a judge will have to take them into account.

Property division is a factor

Another important factor is the way in which your marital property will be divided. Courts must take this into account when awarding alimony or maintenance. Before the divorce, your wife may indeed need a higher weekly amount, because the marital property has yet to be divided. Afterwards, when the house is sold, the bank accounts split, the American Telephone and Telegraph stocks sold and any of your other marital property distributed, your wife may end up with sufficient assets in her own name to warrant reduced alimony or maintenance payments on your part.

Talk it out

Never lose sight of an obvious solution: straightforward discussions with your wife. Explain to her that your original calculations were too optimistic and that financial realities force a cutback in payments. Perhaps another understanding can be reached, one that takes into consideration the true circumstances in which you presently find yourself. The success of this approach depends upon open and honest communication, which is another reason why we counsel clients to refrain from "burning their bridges behind them" just because the marriage relationship has disintegrated. You never know when you will need your spouse's understanding and cooperation.

Often voluntary payments prove impractical. With the advantage of hindsight, you may now view your original decision as a serious economic miscalculation or, even worse, inspired by guilt. After fifteen years of marriage, Joe decided that he *Guilt: im-* had to leave. Neither his wife nor the children understood, but *proper motive* he knew it was necessary. Nevertheless, the strength of his convictions did not completely offset his deep-seated guilt. Before leaving, he told his wife that he would give her $250 each week for her and the children, besides paying for the mortgage and other house expenses. He first moved into a friend's house for a few days. Then he started apartment hunting. He had not had an apartment since he was single, and he could not believe the rents that landlords were now asking. He finally found a small apartment, but after the first month he realized that he was committing economic suicide. Almost three quarters of his take-home pay was going to the support of his wife and children and their home. He could not even pay his own rent without withdrawing money from his savings account. The divorce took a little more than a year. Joe managed, but just barely.

When making any voluntary arrangements for support, be fair to yourself and your spouse. Neither should let emotions rule.

Should I get my wife to sign a writing concerning her agreement to accept $200 per week? Can we do this without a lawyer?

There is seldom a need for a writing at this early stage. An informal agreement is just that, something between you and your wife. Leave it to your lawyers later on down the road to *No need for* work this into a settlement, if that is possible. Concentrate for *writing* now on reaching a fair arrangement and making the payments.

We have already said that these voluntary payments are not controlling. However, even if you went to the trouble of drawing up a contract with your wife, there is little likelihood that it would ever be enforced. Courts look closely at any financial dealings between a husband and wife, especially if they occur

Obligation of fair dealing

during the emotionally trying time of the marital breakup. Any writing that you have her sign is not a simple arm's-length contract, such as one for the purchase of a new home. The marriage relationship implies trust between the parties, something that is never assumed in the marketplace. This trust carries with it an obligation of fair dealing, which can easily be abused by the financially stronger partner. The highly charged atmosphere of an impending divorce cannot help but create fertile ground for fraud, duress, coercion and undue influence,

Suspicion of fraud

as where a husband says, "Unless you sign this, you'll never get a dime from me." Therefore, written agreements signed by spouses, where neither were represented by an attorney, are closely scrutinized and rarely—if ever—automatically followed.

No automatic effect

Whatever you may think of them, judges and lawyers are not naive. They realize that an agreement signed "in the heat of battle" that is not fair and reasonable should not be given judicial effect. In fact, we cannot help but read between the lines and view your question as implying a desire to get away with something. There is really no reason why you should want a writing from your wife. If you want to prove that you made these payments, pay her by check; you will always have the canceled checks to produce in court.

My problem is the other side of the coin. I am afraid that if I do not get a written agreement from my husband, he will renege. Aren't I better protected with something in writing?

Not really. If you think that you need a writing from your

Protection is illusory

and, you are already in trouble. If your husband does not want to pay you anything, it will not matter that he has signed his name on the bottom of the page. We have seen too many spouses ignore court orders and carefully drafted agreements to believe that your home-drawn contract will make any difference.

Right to support is independent from contract

You needn't have a contract to be entitled to support. If your husband is not meeting your financial needs and those of the family, you may seek assistance from the courts, which we discuss in the next section.

Why bother to reach an agreement? Won't the court reach its own conclusion?

That is not the point. Certainly before you get to court something has to be done about the economic realities. The financially dependent spouse will need money. Whether you do it voluntarily or under the mandate of a court order does not change this duty. The difference is that your efforts to arrive at an informal agreement will avoid the necessity of your spouse seeking this court order, which involves needless time and expense for all concerned. Furthermore, there may never even be a need to go to trial. Your informal arrangements may indeed pave the way for an amicable settlement, which will serve everyone well. *Informal agreements save time and money*

TAKING IT TO THE COURTS

Informal discussions and arrangements are the ideal but not necessarily the norm. There are those spouses who for a variety of reasons refuse to recognize their rightful obligations. The dependent spouse need not sit idly by. In fact, the needy spouse does not even have to start a divorce action to obtain monetary relief.

No one likes to contemplate going to court, but a courtroom begins to look a whole lot more inviting if the alternative is pecuniary discomfort or disaster. How to take advantage of your state's judicial mechanisms in order to get such financial assistance is what this section is all about.

My husband moved out over four weeks ago with vague promises to continue to pay the bills and give me spending money. No such luck; I haven't received a cent. Is there a quick way of getting my husband to recognize his financial obligations without having to file for a divorce?

Yes. Every state recognizes that a spouse has financial obligations to his or her family. This does not change because he or she has moved out of the house. You can enforce these obligations in court without commencing a divorce action. This is known as a *support proceeding*, and every state has a procedure whereby you can commence one without filing for a divorce. *Starting a support proceeding*

Although the procedure differs from state to state, most courts enable you to initiate the support proceeding yourself without the assistance of an attorney. Of course, you may first consider whether you want and can afford a lawyer at this stage. The first thing to do is to determine which court to go to. Some states and cities have separate family courts; other states have family court as a division of a particular civil or county court. You can obtain this information easily by calling any court in your state.

Personal interview and mediation services

Most courts assign court personnel to interview and assist you. Sometimes there is a special department that attempts to mediate a settlement before the proceeding is commenced. Someone may telephone or write to your husband at his home or job and explain that unless he begins to make voluntary payments he will be brought involuntarily into court. In any event, come to court prepared. Make sure that you have at your fingertips all of the pertinent financial information. The best thing you can do is prepare a neatly written or typed summary of all your expenses and sources of income, including savings and checking accounts. If possible, bring in as much verification as you can. It is also a good idea to take a copy of your husband's paycheck stub or a copy of last year's joint income tax return. Make sure you also have your husband's full address and telephone number, as well as those of his employer.

Summarize expenses

Support petition

You will be assisted in drawing up a petition or complaint which succinctly sets forth your needs for support. The court usually issues a summons or writ, which in some states is signed by a judge. The summons and petition are then delivered to your husband, either personally or by mail, or both. He is directed to appear at a hearing at a certain time, place and date. If he does not appear, a bench warrant for his arrest may be issued.

What if on the hearing date he comes in with a lawyer? I cannot afford one, and I am no Perry Mason. Won't I be at a disadvantage?

Court-appointed attorney

No. There are two reasons. First, if you want an attorney and cannot afford one, the courts in most states will provide a lawyer at no cost. In large cities, lawyers remain on staff for such duty. When you are first interviewed by someone at the court, make sure you explain that you cannot afford an attorney and wish to have one assigned. Sometimes you will meet the lawyer that day, other times it will not be until the hearing date. Even if you do not bring this out in your interview, you can still make your request to the judge at the hearing. He or she will adjourn the proceeding until a lawyer can be appointed for you.

Second, these support proceedings are usually very informal. *Hearings are* They are designed to obviate the need for lawyers. In fact, we *informal* have seen one or two cases where an attorney did more harm than good by making the proceeding unnecessarily long and drawn out. You do not have to be a Perry Mason. You just have to state what your needs are.

I need money now. How long does a support proceeding take?

Court calendars vary from state to state, city to city and county to county. Nevertheless, support proceedings have pri- *Quick deci-* ority. Even in congested New York City, the time from inter- *sions* view to hearing is usually only a few short weeks. Of course, in large cities, expect that there will be a few adjournments along the way. However, you should have a determination within a month or two.

I've just been served with a court petition requiring my presence in connection with my wife's demand that I pay child support and alimony. Since our separation I have been out of work and I can hardly support myself, let alone pay for a lawyer to defend me against my wife's claim. Can I defend myself against her legal action without hiring an attorney?

Certainly. The informality of support proceedings works as well for you as it does for the petitioning spouse. By the same token, you may be entitled to have a lawyer appointed *Assignment of* for you, and this is something that you can explore by calling *counsel* the court. Very often the phone number is right there on the summons. Even if you are not entitled to free legal counsel, you may be able to find an attorney whose fees will be reasonable.

If you decide to go it alone, be prepared to prove that you are out of work. Take a letter of discharge or a pink slip, records of unemployment payments or anything else that will show your unemployment status. Of course, your unemploy- *Independent* ment only suspends, but does not terminate, your support ob- *corroboration* ligation. The court can make an order requiring you to com- *of job loss* mence payments as soon as you are rehired. We suggest you notify both your wife and the court voluntarily once you get a new job.

My husband is unemployed. I know he quit his job so he wouldn't have to pay me and the kids anything. He is an excellent computer programer, and there are plenty of jobs out there for him. Is there anything I can do about this?

Yes. Commence the support proceeding. You will be entitled to demonstrate at the hearing the fact that your husband is goldbricking and that there are viable job opportunities awaiting him. A spouse's earnings *potential* is a key ingredient in any support decision.

Earning potential important factor

Showing this is not as difficult as it may first seem. Remember, we keep saying the judges are not naive. Since the hearings are informal, you can introduce pages from your newspaper's classified ads offering positions for which your husband is qualified. Your husband's former employer may be brought to testify as to the circumstances surrounding his recent resignation. If he does not wish to appear voluntarily, you can have the court subpoena him. You may even be able to enlist the services of a representative of an employment agency, one who can testify that jobs for which your husband is qualified abound in your area and that someone with his experience and training could expect a lucrative position.

Proving your case

Does this mean that the judge will order my husband to take a job?

No. No judge has that power; this is still a free country. However, the judge can order that your husband pay support as if he had one of these jobs. It will be up to your husband to figure out how he will get the money to make these payments. If he does not make them, he can be held in contempt of court. Contempt carries with it many sanctions, including arrest.

No forced labor

I am a little confused. Sometimes you have talked about motions for temporary support and at other times you talk about a separate support proceeding. What is the difference?

When we talk about motions or applications for temporary support, we speak of something that is in the context of an ongoing divorce action. Once divorce papers are served, either party can make a motion to the court for such pretrial relief. Support proceedings, on the other hand, are independent of a divorce, and they are designed for a situation where a spouse needs support but where no divorce action has commenced. The underlying right for support remains the same. Only the labels and legal procedures are different.

Same right, different procedure

ENFORCING SUPPORT
OR MAINTENANCE ORDERS

Obtaining a temporary order of support may not necessarily be the end of the line for some unfortunate spouses. Although it is printed on a piece of paper and even signed by a judge, a court order, alas, is not money; you cannot pay for the groceries with it. It is not uncommon for some people to disregard a court order, just as they do "No Parking" signs and credit card bills. In such instances, it will be necessary for the other spouse to take advantage of those enforcement devices that assure compliance with the order.

Last month I went into court and succeeded in having the court order my husband to pay me $100 weekly for support. He made the first payment, but he has not paid a dime since then. How do I put "teeth" into the court order?

Enforcing compliance with a court order is a complex subject, one of the most difficult that a matrimonial attorney can face. Fortunately there are special procedures of which you may take advantage to help assure that you receive the support from your husband if he refuses to pay it voluntarily. A support order can be used like a judgment, which means that you can seize your husband's assets or freeze his bank account. This is a relatively simple procedure that your lawyer can initiate. If your husband still refuses to make the payments, you will obtain the money from the sale of his assets at auction or the release of the funds in his bank account directly to you. Another procedure that is often utilized is to "intercept" money owed to your husband by third persons. For instance, three years ago when he sold his hardware store he agreed to take the payments in installments over ten years; you can get a court order that will direct the new owners to make all or a portion of these payments directly to you. *Enforcement devices*

Sale of assets at auction

The disobedience of any court order results in a contempt citation. If it continues, a judge can order the arrest of your husband. Usually this will not be done without first giving him an opportunity to make the payments, but if he remains recalcitrant he may eventually find himself in jail. *Possibility of contempt and arrest*

Sometimes the support order itself has built-in protections, either requiring that your husband make the support payments directly to the court or containing a payroll deduction order.

What is a payroll deduction order?

Payroll deduction

This is a court order that is served directly on your husband's employer, directing the employer to deduct a certain portion of his wages and pay them by separate check either to you or directly to the court. A payroll deduction order may apply to part or all of the support due you each week.

My wife got a payroll deduction order about a year ago. Every payday my boss complains what a pain in the neck it is for his bookkeeper. Can I do anything to get out from under this?

Once in place, not easily removed

A payroll deduction order is not lightly granted. It is usually a last resort, used where a judge finds bad faith on your part or a history of non-payment. Consequently, it is not easily discharged. You will have to convince the court not only of a change of heart but that there exists some other security for your payments.

May have to put up collateral

You should consult with an attorney and explore the possibility of making an application to modify your wife's support order. You can request that the judge allow you to make the payments directly to your wife. Most times, the judge will require that you either post a bond or some other asset, such as a savings passbook, as collateral, just in case you do not make good on your word. This protects your wife until the payroll deduction order can be reinstated should you again miss a payment or two. After sufficient time has elapsed, you may be able to make another application for the release of the collateral, showing that you have been making the payments regularly and on time.

I can't make these payments anymore to my husband. He is threatening to put me in jail, but what good would that do? Isn't that just like debtor's prison?

Specter of debtor's prison

In a sense, yes. There is logically no causal relationship between putting someone in jail and producing income. However, we have seen that it often works magic, and sudden, heretofore undisclosed sources of income spring up from nowhere. Arrest is coercive, not income-producing.

There have been many constitutional attacks on the practice of locking up a non-paying spouse. However, in most states the procedure survives, and it is sometimes the only method that can be employed to ensure that payments are made. We may not necessarily condone the practice, but we cannot argue with the results. The deprivation of one's liberty is not taken lightly, and judges will only order an arrest as the very last resort. This *Arrest and* is especially so if the judge perceives that the spouse is holding *detention as* back from disclosing all of his or her income or is being openly *last resort* defiant. If you really do not have the money, you will not spend your life in prison. You may even be released after only one day, but who really wants to go through the experience?

If you truly cannot meet the support obligation, do not wait until the sheriff takes you away in handcuffs. Instead, initiate your own proceeding to modify the prior court order. Just as *Taking the in-* your spouse came to court with proof of his needs, prepare *itiative* your own evidence to show that you are unable to continue making these payments. The court would then order a reduction in the support obligations instead of your arrest. Arrest will only happen to those who let a long period elapse and continue to ignore the mandates of the court.

I have never missed one support payment, but last week I lost my job. I tried to explain the situation to my wife, but she says that if I don't come up with the money by next week she is going to start enforcement proceedings. If I am brought into court, will the fact that I lost my job be taken into consideration by the judge?

Of course. Changed circumstances are always significant. Support orders are not etched in stone, and they are always *Modifying* subject to upward or downward modification. *prior orders*

Make sure that the judge is advised by you or your lawyer that you are unemployed, through no fault of your own. Second, be prepared to testify as to all of your good-faith attempts to find new employment. We have already seen what can hap- *Be prepared* pen with a goldbricker. If the judge is satisfied that the reason *to show your* for your unemployment is valid and that your efforts to obtain *efforts to find* a new job are legitimate, he will have no choice but to reduce *work* or even suspend the support payments until you re-enter the job market.

It may be advisable for you to commence your own proceeding before your wife goes into court. This will show your *Start your* sincerity and take away some of her thunder. In enforcement *own proceed-* proceedings, judges expect a thousand and one excuses from *ing* the spouse being brought involuntarily to court, and your story may get a better review if you are the one initiating the proceeding. Of course, just because you lost your job does not mean an automatic reduction in your support obligation. You may have savings or income-producing assets. If your wife and

Many factors considered

children are totally dependent on your income, you may have to sell the Ferrari. Or the Chevy, as the case may be. Your proof in the proceeding will be the same, showing your expenses, the reason you lost your job and your attempts to get a new one.

I've just been notified that my wife is bringing me into court for my failure to keep up with my weekly child support payments. What if I just don't show up on the court date?

"Cutting class" not recommended

Don't be foolish, for you may very well show up for the next court date in handcuffs. If you do not appear for the hearing, the judge can issue a bench warrant, something which he or she will not hesitate to do in a support proceeding. This is just like an arrest. You will be picked up by a sheriff or police officer wherever and whenever you can be found. You will either be brought directly to the court or sometimes locked up until the court is next in session. If you cannot make that particular hearing for legitimate reasons, such as a business trip or ill health, make sure that you or your attorney contact and advise

Obtaining adjournment for good cause

the court of the situation. You will always be given an adjournment for reasonable cause. Only your silence and seemingly willful refusal to appear can lead to trouble. If you do not have a lawyer, you can contact the court directly, but we suggest you also follow it up with a letter, such as:

Family Court, Support Section
Room 410
New York, New York 10013
　　Re: Docket No. 46-3214/81
　　　Shiela Brown vs. Gregory Brown

Dear Sir/Madam:

Sample letter to court

This is in confirmation of our telephone conversation earlier today, whereby I confirmed receipt of the summons and petition in the above proceeding and requested an adjournment of the court hearing date, originally scheduled for September 10, 1982, at 9:30 A.M. in room 506.

As we discussed, I will be out of town that week at a sales convention in Toledo, Ohio. I expect to return the night of September 25, 1982. In this regard, I enclose a copy of a letter from my employer confirming same. Kindly notify me in writing of the time and date of the adjourned hearing.

Thank you for your assistance and attention to this matter.

Yours truly,
Gregory Brown

In some large cities, you may find that it is impossible to get an adjournment without having someone appear in court on your behalf on that hearing day. If you will be out of town, we *Retaining a* suggest that you retain an attorney immediately for this pur- *stand-in* pose. Make it clear in your initial conversation with the lawyer that you are only retaining his or her services to obtain an adjournment, and the fee should be set accordingly.

My husband's payments came for the first couple of months, but now he seems to have disappeared. How can I expect to enforce the support order when I can't even find my husband? Any advice?

Your husband may have left town, but some of his assets may have been left behind. You would then be able to obtain an *order of sequestration.* A sheriff or other court officer would *Locate assets* then be entitled to seize these assets and deliver them to you. *left behind* Of course, the ideal asset is a bank account. Otherwise you will have to sell the property.

Unfortunately, many spouses disappear without leaving any assets. Our court system and the protection of our laws then begin to break down. The police will not put out an all-points *System* bulletin. Any efforts to locate your spouse will have to be done *breakdown* by you or a private detective. The latter is prohibitively expensive for most. All we can suggest is that you constantly telephone his friends and relatives, asking not only for his whereabouts but even their intervention in making him come to his senses.

I got my support order from the court and there were no problems with payment until my husband moved out of state to Florida. Do I now have to go to Florida to enforce the order, or is there a way that I can enforce it here in Michigan?

You are in luck. All fifty states have adopted a version of the Uniform Reciprocal Enforcement of Support Act (URESA). *Adoption of* The purpose of this act is to compel support of dependent *URESA by* spouses and children outside of the home state and to provide a *all states* procedure for the enforcement of support against persons residing in other states or territories without the necessity of having to go to that state to initiate the proceeding. Therefore, you can go to your own court in Michigan and start the ball rolling there. That court will then refer your case to an appropriate court in Florida. The information that you provide to your home court will be transmitted to the court in Florida and

Your petition is transmitted out of state

become the basis for a petition that will be served on your husband. Not only will the Florida court hear your case, it will appoint an attorney to prosecute it on your behalf. It is just as if you were in Florida yourself.

Your husband will be notified of the proceeding in Florida, where he will defend against your petition if he so chooses. If the facts in your petition are sufficient to warrant an order of support, the Florida court will direct one against your husband. In all likelihood, he will make the payments directly to the Florida court, which will then send them either to you or the Michigan court. As you can imagine, the procedure does take a little time, but it has proven effective in many instances. Finally, if your husband refuses to obey the order, the Florida court can bring against him essentially the same enforcement proceedings as you could have brought in Michigan. For example, they may order a payroll deduction or attach his bank account.

Payments to court

Of course, if circumstances permit, you may decide to prosecute your claim in Florida. This is accomplished by contacting an attorney in that state who will represent your interests. However, this option is often too expensive for many people to consider, and in addition it requires your presence in Florida at some point during the proceeding—a requirement that you may find to be entirely unfeasible.

Prosecuting your own case

Chapter Four
CHOOSING A LAWYER

The decision to divorce your spouse is the first critical one. Selecting an attorney to represent you is the second. The greater the number of issues—maintenance, property division and child custody/support—involved in your case, the more important the choice becomes. Just because Ms. Ipso Facto did the house closing four years ago does not necessarily mean that she is the best bet now for your divorce, which is becoming an increasingly specialized area in many parts of the country.

Courts possess broad powers today that go well beyond the traditional role of dissolving the marriage and awarding child support and alimony. Under the equitable or community property division laws enacted in most states (see Appendix), courts can now award specific interests in property and other assets acquired during the marriage by either spouse and fashion all types of innovative relief: a wife in New Jersey ends up with a choice cut of her husband's partnership interest in the butcher shop; a husband in New York is ordered to maintain a $75,000 life insurance policy for his kids. Not only developments in the law but societal changes as well have resulted in making divorce litigation more complex. Where years ago the custody of the children was assumed from the beginning to belong to the wife, more and more husbands today are pressing claims for exclusive or joint custody, largely because men have begun to assume a more active and accepted role in child care. Consequently, the attorney's role becomes ever more important.

Finding an attorney is difficult. No rating system exists; win/loss records are not maintained in the local courthouse.

Moreover, an attorney's record of success is but one element to consider. Because you will certainly be working closely together in the ensuing months, you must also have confidence and trust in his or her abilities, and you should be able to confide in one another and get along. Finally, many lawyers despise divorces. They may be otherwise excellent litigators, but they lack the requisite stamina to put up with the emotional conflicts inherent in most matrimonial actions. On the other hand, some attorneys are psychologically fit but legally inept.

Your choice will in the final analysis be based more on instinct than reason—the "feeling" you have for a particular attorney. Nevertheless, it is possible to make a more rational decision by carefully considering and specifying your needs and by utilizing the various and often excellent sources of referral.

WHAT TO LOOK FOR

Nowhere is it more important to shop—not necessarily for price but for competency and compassion. The choice of attorney can have a very direct, and sometimes profound, effect on the ultimate settlement or award. Remember, the legal termination of the marriage—the divorce—is but one element. More importantly, the financial, property and custodial rights that are established may have far more bearing on your future than the fact that you are no longer married.

Is there such a thing as a matrimonial specialist?

Misleading term

The term *specialist* is somewhat misleading. There are actually very few recognized specialties in the legal field. Most states will only certify an attorney as a specialist in such areas as patents and admiralty. However, there are attorneys who tend to confine their practice to a particular area of the law, such as divorce and family law.

Trend is to specialize

Because new laws are promulgated almost every year, and a plethora of decisions are handed down each day by the courts, the trend in the legal profession is toward specialization. An attorney must keep abreast of these developments, and no one is capable of doing so for every area of the law. Consequently, more and more attorneys confine themselves to one or two areas of practice, so as to enable them to provide the best services for their clients. This is nowhere more true than in the area of matrimonial law.

It used to be that almost any attorney could adequately handle a divorce. However, with the advent of community property or equitable distribution laws and the changing economic realities of our times, the various phases of a divorce case are *Plethora of* necessarily more complex, demanding specific expertise. A *issues* matrimonial lawyer must be able to deal with such issues as tax ramifications, pensions, the economic value of homemaking services, actuary tables and other financially related topics, while at the same time retaining the emotional stamina to offer sound advice concerning marital fault issues and custody disputes.

Because most courts now treat marriage as "an economic partnership," the financial side of the divorce plays a much larger role than ever before. More time is required for proper pretrial preparation. In all but the fewest cases, extensive financial disclosure and discovery is necessary. The attorney must know what to look for and where to look for it. A court *Financial dis-* cannot divide property that it does not know exists, and it is *closure is cru-* therefore incumbent upon an attorney to discover all assets *cial* and bring them to the attention of the court. The bigger the pie, the bigger the slice. Failure to discover important assets prior to trial can have disastrous, irreversible consequences later. This is where expertise in this area may be critical to your case.

A lawyer told me that he is a member of "the Matrimonial Bar." What does this mean?

The word "Bar" is only shorthand for *Bar Association,* a sort of trade association for attorneys. Every attorney in good standing and admitted to practice before the courts of his or her state may become a member of a Bar Association; it is usually only a matter of paying dues. Within each Bar Association there are divisions which attorneys who practice in a given area of the law can join. Invariably, a Bar Association will have a section made up primarily of those attorneys practicing matrimonial and family law; it is a way of exchanging ideas and helping one another keep abreast of changes and trends in *Lawyers'* the law. However, a lawyer who is a member of the so-called *trade associa-* Matrimonial Bar does not necessarily have any more skills, *tion* competence or experience than his colleagues who have never been inside the Bar Association building. On the other hand, it is a positive factor to consider, for it indicates a serious interest and commitment to the area of matrimonial law.

My neighbor told me that he got his divorce by going to "a bomber." What is he talking about?

Not an airplane. The term refers to a certain style and approach, one which is becoming less prevalent. A bomber is an attorney who prides himself or herself on projecting and maintaining the proverbial "tough guy" image, playing the heavy. He or she sees divorce as open warfare and is much more comfortable with high-altitude saturation bombing than with surgically precise air strikes. The bomber believes that the client is best served by intimidation—this includes you, the adversary and often the judge—and that you have retained him or her to "kill" your spouse.

Tough-guy approach

Sometimes this approach serves clients well, and this undoubtedly is the underlying reason for the high fees that bombers frequently command. This was especially true in the days when marital fault played an important role in the outcome of a divorce. For example, in New York prior to 1967, the only ground or basis for divorce was adultery. If you wanted a divorce you sometimes really did need a lawyer who would be willing to have someone on hand who didn't think twice about smashing through motel doors and quickly taking a few compromising photographs. Intimidating witnesses on the stand often proved successful, and bombastic courtroom techniques flourished. Moreover, when the only financial issue at stake was alimony, the size of the figure the judge was likely to award depended on how dramatic a picture the wife's attorney could paint.

Relies upon intimidation

These days, most divorce trials have all the excitement and tension of a bankruptcy proceeding. With the issue of marital fault relegated to the background in most states, the only important testimony concerns the couple's assets and expenses. Can you imagine your lawyer shouting over an income tax return or a bank statement? Often a more level-headed, clinical approach gets better results. The task is now cutting the pie, not throwing it.

My friend says I need a lawyer who is sympathetic. My grocer says that I need "a killer." A neighbor has volunteered that I should look for a negotiator. With all this advice, I'm getting confused. Any suggestions?

The choice of an attorney for a divorce action is critical. This is the one time that you play judge, so be sure to make the most of it. You should consider many factors, but it really comes down to choosing a person with whom you are comfortable, one whose style and approach jibes with yours. *Choosing a lawyer*

Nearly everyone seeks a sympathetic attorney. After all, this is a divorce, not a house closing. However, you must be careful that your lawyer is not so sympathetic that he or she begins to identify with your plight, losing the requisite objectivity. If you feel that you need a lawyer who can respond to your emotional needs, you should discuss this at your initial conference and ascertain whether that lawyer will indeed be available for your inevitable evening telephone call. A good matrimonial lawyer has to have a working knowledge of psychology, taxes, real estate and stocks, as well as the divorce laws and procedures of your particular state. The best lawyer is one who will not only work for you but *with* you. *Shouldn't identify too closely*

We have already discussed the so-called "killers" or "bombers." If you need the trauma and emotional release that they sometimes provide, then perhaps this is what you should look for. On the other side of the scale is the negotiator, one who prides himself or herself on an ability to settle cases before they go to trial. This is certainly a laudatory goal, but you should look carefully to make sure that it does not signal a fear or hesitancy to go to court. Although the vast majority of divorces are settled before trial, the sad truth is that a sizable number still require a full hearing. If an adversary gets a sense that your lawyer is afraid to go to trial, he or she will likely take a much harder line. *Beware of gun-shy attorneys*

I had a great lawyer who negotiated the sale of my business a few years ago, and I would like to hire him again. How can I judge his competence in the area of matrimonial law?

We have already explained that divorce has become more complex and that many lawyers are now unfamiliar with the new trends and procedures that have evolved in this area. This is not to say that your lawyer does not have the requisite experience and ability, but you should interview him anew about his specific experience in matrimonial law before making your decision. You already have the advantage of knowing how it is *Interview lawyer* to work with him. The days of the general practitioner are unfortunately going the way of the dinosaur.

WHERE TO GO

You may have an idea of the type of lawyer you want, but not the slightest notion where to look. You are hardly alone. Lawyers may exist by the thousands, yet finding the right one can be an arduous, if not impossible, task. Only recently have attorneys been permitted to advertise; however, very few do. Most still rely on the tried and true "word of mouth" method and referrals from other lawyers to obtain clients. As litigious as our society is reputed to be, relatively few people have ever dealt with a trial attorney before their divorce; many wind up retaining the brother-in-law of the guy across the street for want of any better recommendation.

There are various ways to find a competent attorney. The particularity of your case will to some extent influence your methods. Most individuals require only competent and reasonably priced representation, which can be obtained in a number of ways. Others need high-priced specialists, whom they are unlikely to find by blindly sticking a finger into the yellow pages.

Just what are the available means and methods of finding a competent and reasonably priced attorney?

The best way of finding an attorney is through a referral from a trusted friend, relative or another attorney. There is no one better than a former client to attest to the ability of an attorney. You may have friends who have gone through a divorce, so start by asking them about their experiences. Also check with any attorneys whom you know who may be able to refer you to a colleague with specific expertise in the area.

First try to get a personal referral

Then try your local Bar Association

The second step in your approach should be to contact your local Bar Association. Most of them have a referral service at little or no charge.

I called my local Bar Association last evening and was given the name of an attorney who was on the Association's Matrimonial Bar referral list. I'm curious; how does an attorney get on the list? Is there a screening process, and if so, what does it consist of?

The rules for every Bar Association vary, but generally each requires a minimum period for an attorney to be practicing law before he or she can be placed on the list. An attorney who is *Attorney vol-* interested in being listed simply volunteers and often fills out a *unteers* detailed application that elicits various information, including areas of legal expertise. Often a face-to-face interview follows, after which time the attorney's name is placed on the list. Most Bar Associations either rotate the list or select a name at random when an individual requests a lawyer for a particular purpose.

Since matrimonial law is not a recognized specialty in most states, there is really no process by which an attorney's self-stated qualifications can be verified. If there is any screening *Limited* process, it is usually devoted to inquiring into the attorney's *screening* record to determine if any grievances or complaints have been filed against him or her. Seldom is there any further investigation or follow-up inquiries. There is, however, a practical control mechanism. Obviously, if the Bar Association receives numerous complaints about a particular attorney, it is safe to assume that that attorney's name will be deleted from the referral list.

How do Bar referral services work? Do I have to pay a fee for the referral?

You simply telephone your local Bar Association and request that you be referred to a lawyer. You will then be interviewed by someone, often a lawyer, who will ascertain the na- *Dial-a-lawyer* ture of your problem and the type of legal representation that you require. In your case, the matrimonial list would be consulted, and you would be given the names and telephone numbers of lawyers in your geographical area.

You next contact those attorneys whose names you were given, explaining that you have been referred to them by the Bar Association. Often there is a special procedure whereby referral attorneys agree to meet with you and charge a substantially lower fee for the initial consultation. In some in- *Consultation* stances, they do not keep this fee; instead they send it to the *fee minimal* Bar Association, which helps defray the expense of the service. You will explain your problem at your consultation, at which time the attorney will usually quote you his or her fee. Of course, you do not have to retain this lawyer, and you may first want to consult with some of the other names that you have.

My union has a prepaid legal plan. How does this system work?

Prepaid legal plans usually take two forms, the *closed panel* and the *open panel*. There is also a hybrid approach that combines features of both.

Closed panel; staff attorneys

The closed panel plan consists of retaining a staff of in-house attorneys to handle all consultations and legal representation in covered categories. These categories usually include standard legal services such as house closings, landlord-tenant problems, wills and simple bankruptcies. Most plans also include the category of matrimonial proceedings. Attorneys in the closed panel approach are usually paid by the union or the company and, hence, the client need not pay legal fees.

Open panel; designated outside attorneys

The open panel plan permits the individual members to choose their own counsel, and then the union or company reimburses all or part of the legal costs incurred for certain specified types of cases covered by the plan. The choice of attorneys is usually limited to those on a list provided to the member.

Hybrid plan

The hybrid plan provides an in-house staff of lawyers for the initial consultations and conferences. If the staff lawyer cannot dispense with the matter easily and quickly, he or she then provides the member with a list of attorneys. The member will then be entitled to reimbursement of a portion or all of the legal fees paid to the attorney chosen from the list.

Explore it first

Prepaid legal services plans have been both criticized and applauded. Much of the success depends on the particular plan. If your company or union has such a plan and you are eligible for it, then we suggest that you explore the possibility of using it. At the very least, a prepaid legal services plan offers you another means of finding an attorney whom you feel comfortable with. Check it out—you have nothing to lose.

I see that more and more attorneys are advertising in the newspapers. Their fees seem quite modest, but my buddy claims that if they were so good they wouldn't have to advertise. What are your feelings on advertising as a means of finding a lawyer?

As you are probably aware, legal advertising is fairly new, having been permitted only several years ago by the U.S. Supreme Court. In some states, the content of the advertisement is closely regulated. Generally, lawyers are restricted to advertising their fees and the types of services they provide; no *Legal adver-* claims can be made for extraordinary ability or success for- *tising is a new* mulas. Given these restrictions, the only real inducement that *concept* any advertisement can offer over another is a lower fee.

Attorneys who advertise low fees obviously anticipate a volume business. They rely as much as possible on prepared *Volume busi-* forms, questionnaires and paralegals, i.e., trained legal assis- *ness* tants who are not attorneys. All this is designed to reduce the amount of time that an attorney has to devote to your case. The system seems to work very well for routine legal matters, such as house closings and bankruptcies. It can also work for *Works best* undefended divorces where there is little at stake, as, for in- *for routine* stance, the divorce of two people married several years with no *matters* children and modest assets. The disadvantages are self-evident. There is less personal contact with a lawyer. If your case is not routine and develops some snags, the office may not be able to cope with it. Finally, for special or complex matters, such as *Less personal* tax and child custody issues, there may not be the necessary *contact* counseling and expertise available.

Some attorneys do not specify fees in their advertisements. For them, advertising is another way of making their name known in the community. It is similar to attending meetings at the Kiwanis Club. These attorneys will usually quote their fees *Advertising* over the telephone, or at least set up a consultation at little or *"reasonable* no cost. Your friend's negative assumptions about attorneys *fees"* who advertise may not necessarily be valid. There are many fine attorneys with years of experience who find advertising a legitimate means of exposure. Many are sincerely interested in offering adequate representation to the community at reasonable prices.

If you decide to consult with an attorney who advertises, interview him or her in the same manner as you would anyone else who is about to represent you. Ask those questions that you feel are important, even if some will make you feel a little awkward. Evaluate carefully the stated qualifications of your *Evaluate law-* prospective lawyer. He or she may claim to have handled well *yer's claims* over a hundred divorces, but it may turn out that most of those were undefended, with few issues at stake. Perhaps he or she has never actually conducted a divorce trial. If your situation is complex and requires personal attention and experience, you must assure yourself that this attorney will be capable of delivering the services that you require.

I saw an ad on television the other night for a legal clinic. What's the story with legal clinics? Are they a good bet?

Once again, the answer depends upon the complexity of your case. There are several large legal clinics that have opened offices throughout the country. They are usually able to offer adequate services at reduced fees because of the cost savings inherent in their pooling resources and standardizing procedures. These clinics hire local managing attorneys, usually one or two years out of law school, and rely on a number of paralegals and clerical staff. The emphasis is on volume and routine legal matters, such as house closings and wills.

Standardized services

Some clinics will also handle a contested divorce, charging the client hourly fees. A recent survey in the New York Metropolitan area revealed that these fees are not necessarily any less than those charged by small local firms and single practitioners. So you should investigate these other alternatives before retaining a clinic on the strength of television advertising and claims of "affordability."

Fees not necessarily lower

I've heard that in some situations a person can do his or her own divorce. In fact, I have seen divorce "kits" advertised in the paper. What is this all about?

The procedure for obtaining an undefended divorce has been simplified in most states, especially in those that have eliminated the requisite fault grounds for divorce. The parties do not even have to appear in court in most instances, and relatively simple legal papers are submitted to a judge or referee for signature. It is not that surprising, therefore, that some enterprising companies have compiled and organized the necessary paperwork into standardized forms called "divorce kits," complete with instructions. All you do is fill in the blanks, pay the filing fee and file the papers with the court. The divorce may take anywhere between two and fifteen weeks, depending on your jurisdiction. The procedure is simple and inexpensive.

Fill-in-the-blank forms

We cannot overemphasize that "do-it-yourself" divorces are only suitable in situations where there is a marriage of relatively short duration (a few years), there are no children, there is no property or substantial assets to be divided and the parties are in full agreement as to the elements of the divorce. In any other case, these kits fall woefully short of meeting the needs of the parties. This is especially true for the financially dependent spouse. If you have even the slightest doubt that

Use only for simple divorces

your situation may not be so straightforward, the best thing you can do is to consult first with an attorney.

You have mentioned "undefended divorces." What are those?

An undefended divorce is obtained by one spouse against the other on the basis of the latter not appearing or responding in the court proceeding. Essentially it is a default judgment. A *Default judgment* divorce is a civil action, and is started by the service of a summons. The procedure varies from state to state, but there is a limited time period for the *defendant*—the person upon whom the summons is served—to respond and contest the divorce. If that time lapses, the person seeking the divorce—the *plaintiff*—is entitled to file papers with the court and obtain an undefended divorce.

Many couples mistakenly assume that their divorce should be undefended because both parties want a divorce. However, there may be other issues that should be contested, or at least *Other issues* resolved, before the papers are filed with the court. These in- *may be contested* clude maintenance, child support, child custody and division *tested* of marital property. What most lawyers do in such instances is try to reach a settlement between the parties, who then sign an agreement, called a *stipulation* or *settlement*. The terms reached by the parties will control and become part of the provisions contained in the final divorce decree.

If you are served with a summons, never ignore it unless you are willing not only to let your spouse get a divorce but also to *Look before* allow him or her to dictate its terms. If there are no issues, *you default* there are no terms to dictate, and dissolving the marriage is a relatively simple task. On the other hand, if there are certain issues that you would like resolved or agreed upon, you must take action, the first step being a consultation with an attorney.

My wife and I have everything worked out. Do we need our own separate lawyers, or can we have just one lawyer represent us?

You will both require separate lawyers. It is unethical and a conflict of interest for any attorney to represent both parties in a divorce, even where everything has been worked out and agreed upon beforehand. The concerns of each party are dif- *Conflict of interest* ferent. For example, the perspective of one agreeing to pay *terest* support will be different from the one who will be receiving it. One lawyer cannot wear two hats and try to advise each independently.

Well, if the lawyer can only represent one of us, do I need a lawyer or can I do it alone?

Nothing stops you from representing yourself. In fact, in some instances where the parties are essentially in agreement, only one spouse will retain a lawyer to handle the divorce. The other spouse will then sign a *waiver* stating that he or she was informed of the right and advisability of retaining separate counsel, but that he or she waived that right freely and voluntarily. As long as the terms are essentially fair and the unrepresented spouse can fully understand the legal and practical implications, any agreement between the parties will be upheld, and the divorce upon which it is based will be valid. However, there is always a risk to both sides when one party is not represented. The party who acts as his own lawyer may unknowingly give up certain rights. Meanwhile, the other spouse may end up with an agreement or divorce that could later be found by a court to be invalid because of the unbalanced representation.

We would like to digress a moment and point out that when we say that a person may be unknowingly giving up certain rights by foregoing an attorney, we do not at the same time wish to discourage amicable or mediated divorce settlements. We believe that in many instances the parties themselves are fully capable of determining the elements of their divorce. A lawyer in such a case need only act as a sounding board and informal adviser, and he or she should be very circumspect and not stir things up unnecessarily. Rather, the task is to advise the client of all available rights provided by statute and case law and then allow the client to make his or her own decision. All we insist upon is that your decision be a knowing and considered one.

Waiving counsel

Terms must be fair and reasonable

Amicable and mediated divorce settlements

WHAT TO ASK ABOUT FEES

At this point, you should be getting the idea that a divorce can be a time-consuming proposition. To an attorney, time equals money. Sometimes the numbers in the equation can be startling, so it is important that you and your prospective attorney discuss the matter of fees in the initial interview. There are various ways in which a fee is set, and even in which it is paid. However, we always suggest that your particular arrangement be summarized in a simple written retainer agreement.

You say a divorce can take a long time. How much is it going to cost me?

Don't ask us, ask your lawyer. Each case is different. Some lawyers charge more than others. The methods of fixing the fee vary. *Ask your lawyer*

The nature and extent of a couple's assets and income and the possibility of controverted issues, such as child custody, are all taken into account by an attorney in estimating a fee. Obviously a divorce involving two young people who have only been married three years and are both employed and have no assets to speak of will be much easier to handle and consume less time than one featuring a twenty-year marriage, four children and considerable assets, including a family business. Fees will be set accordingly. *Complexity of case*

There are no longer any set fees for an attorney's services. There used to be minimal fee schedules distributed to attorneys by the local Bar Association; however, these were invalidated several years ago by the U.S. Supreme Court. Consequently, an attorney can charge whatever he or she feels is appropriate. An attorney with more experience or reputation in the field will generally charge more. We recommend that you question a prospective attorney as to his or her background in the matrimonial field. If you are going to consult with a high-priced expert, you should first determine whether the circumstances of your case warrant such a large investment; many other attorneys may be able to do the same thing for considerably less money. We have already pointed out that many routine undefended divorces can be handled adequately by legal clinics. *No set fees* *Consider qualifications*

The final factor is the method by which the fee is calculated. Some attorneys quote a "flat" fee. This is a fixed amount for the particular service to be rendered. An experienced attorney can often estimate to a decent degree of certainty the amount of time that will be required for a particular matter and set a fee based upon the anticipated hours. Very often, this fee is at stated intervals. For example, an attorney may charge an additional sum if the case proceeds to trial. *Flat fees*

Another method that is beginning to be used more frequently in divorces is the hourly fee. The attorney quotes his or her hourly fee, which sometimes differs between in-office time and time needed for court appearances. The attorney then requires an initial retainer covering, in the usual instance, the *Hourly fee* first fifteen or twenty hours. Afterwards, the client is billed for additional time expended. Due to the complexity of many divorces with the advent of equitable distribution laws, attorneys have become more reluctant to set flat fees, and they prefer being remunerated for the specific hours they devote to each case.

How is this hourly fee determined?

Fee varies

There is no rule. It is often what the market will bear for an attorney of given experience and credentials. The "difficulty factor" of your case is also taken into account, and it is not uncommon for an attorney to charge a higher hourly rate for a particularly unusual or complicated case. Practically speaking, a lawyer will also base the hourly rate on an estimation of what you can afford to pay and what is at stake in the action.

But can you be a little more specific? What exactly is the range for divorce fees?

Wide latitude in fee structure

The range is very broad. Fees for a divorce can start at approximately $250 for an undefended divorce, where no issues are at stake, and go all the way up to (or past) $25,000 for a fully contested action that involves substantial marital assets, income and property.

Although there are no statistics to back us up, the median fee for a divorce that goes all the way to trial is somewhere around $5,000.

How do people pay these fees?

Ordinarily attorneys require that the fee or initial retainer be paid "up front." If the attorney is hired on an hourly-fee basis, or with provision for payment in some other incremental fashion, he or she will require that additional payments be made as more time is expended.

Step basis of payment

Depending upon the client's financial circumstances, many attorneys will accept the fee or retainer in several installments, which are usually keyed into the various stages of the litigation. For example, you may be asked to pay an initial retainer of $1,500, another $1,000 upon the service of the complaint and the balance before trial.

What if someone doesn't have the money to retain a lawyer?

Many financially dependent spouses frequently find themselves in the situation where they lack ready cash with which to retain an attorney. While recognizing the seriousness of their plight, most attorneys will still require some sort of substantial *May need to* initial payment. If you lack access to the marital funds, you *borrow* may be forced to borrow the money from friends or relatives. Some people have been known to obtain personal loans or cash advances on their credit.

One word of advice: if you are forced to borrow money from a friend or relative, make sure that you have something in writing indicating that the money was given as a loan and not *Loan vs. gift* as a gift. This way the loan becomes a marital obligation—"a necessary"—for which your spouse may be required to reimburse you at a later date. Also do not forget to tell your lawyer about the loan, so that he or she can include this as part of your claim.

What is the least expensive way of getting divorced?

As we have said before, the more that you and your spouse resolve for yourselves, the less your lawyer fees will be. If you can tell your lawyer at the initial consultation that everything *Less issues,* has been worked out and that your spouse will not contest the *less money* divorce, the fee will be moderate, because your attorney will not have to devote a great deal of time and energy to your case.

Even if you do not have everything resolved by the time you consult an attorney, it still may be possible for the outstanding issues to be worked out with a minimum of negotiation. Ofttimes the mere presence of an outside party is sufficient impetus. Moreover, once your spouse retains an attorney, he or she may become much more reasonable after being advised of his or her legal position and potential exposure.

If negotiations break down and a settlement cannot be reached, you can expect a significant increase in the fees. *Controversy* Rarely will a lawyer commence a divorce action without first *means greater* having obtained a full financial commitment from the client. *fees* This means paying a substantial retainer.

Finally, you may be eligible for free legal counsel. Many cities have a Legal Aid Society that provides representation to *Maybe Legal* clients with absolutely no ability to pay a fee. Unfortunately, *Aid* these programs have, in recent years, been at the mercy of budget cutbacks, and most people find that they are either ineligible or that the waiting period for Legal Aid assistance is prohibitive.

A friend of mine got hurt in an auto accident and he didn't have to pay his lawyer anything. Instead, the lawyer agreed to take one third of whatever they got. Can't the same arrangement be made in a divorce?

You are speaking of what we call a *contingency fee* arrangement, wherein a lawyer agrees to take a fixed percentage of the amount of money recovered on behalf of the client, if any. This is very common in the area of personal injury litigation. Alas, it is unethical in nearly every state for a lawyer to be retained in a divorce action on a contingency basis. Believe us, this is probably as disappointing to divorce attorneys as it is to many clients. We are sure there were lots of cases that were settled for several millions of dollars which the attorneys wished they could have walked away from with one third. On balance, however, the view has evolved that contingency fee arrangements might reward litigation and dissuade lawyers from amicably settling a divorce case due to their personal stake in the outcome.

No contingency fee permitted

I have heard that my husband can be made by the court to pay for my lawyer. How does this work?

In most states, if you do not have the financial ability to afford your own lawyer, your spouse can be made to contribute to that attorney's fee. At one time, a husband was invariably responsible for the expenses of his wife's attorney. This legal concept was a throwback to the days when the wife was usually totally dependent upon the husband's income. If it were not for such a rule, a wife could rarely have afforded an attorney to protect her interests. Now the rule is gender-neutral in most states, and the financially dependent spouse can seek counsel fees regardless of sex.

Traditional view is changing

The procedure varies from state to state. A motion or application for counsel fees is made by your attorney at some point during the case, either before, during or after trial. Your financial circumstances are examined, as is your husband's ability to pay. Counsel fees will not be awarded if the court finds that you can afford them. Other important factors include the complexity and difficulty of the litigation and your attorney's experience and standing in the legal community. If the application is considered after trial, the final results are also taken into consideration.

Application for counsel fees

Nevertheless, you will most likely have to pay your attorney something. Very few take a matrimonial case entirely on speculation, hoping that the court will award a decent fee. Most attorneys will require that an initial retainer be paid, after which *Must pay* they will look to your husband for additional amounts. An at- *something* torney is not required to take your case if you cannot afford to pay him or her.

I've already met with an attorney, and we have agreed to a fee. However, she says the fee does not include "costs and disbursements" or appeals. What does she mean?

Costs and disbursements are expenses incurred during the course of your divorce action. Most courts require filing fees, which in some states can be over $100. Someone must pay the individual who personally delivered the summons to your spouse. There are expenses involved in pretrial discovery, such *Expenses of* as appraiser, investigator or accountant fees or the cost of an *litigation* examination before trial. Some attorneys also include certain office expenses that can directly be attributed to your case, such as postage, telephone calls, copying costs and other miscellaneous expenses. You must pay these costs and disbursements apart from the agreed-upon fee; it is money out of your lawyer's pocket, for which she will seek reimbursement. Just make sure that her definition of costs and disbursements is specifically included in your retainer agreement. Each law firm or attorney is free to set their own policy, so your lawyer should explain hers at the initial conference.

The fee for appeals is rarely included in your basic retainer. *Fee for ap-* At certain points during the litigation or after the final deci- *peals separate* sion, either party may decide to appeal all or part of the court's determination.

Jane was awarded $70 per week in a pretrial motion for temporary child support. She felt that this was inadequate, and her lawyer appealed the decision to the next highest court. The original award was modified, and Jane's husband was made to pay $90 each week. Jane's lawyer charged her an additional $2,500 for preparing and arguing the appeal. You can take out your pocket calculator and determine whether it was worth it. There are also certain costs and disbursements inherent in an appeal, the most expensive of which is the printing of the appellate brief and record. This can often run into several hundred dollars, if not thousands when a trial is appealed.

What are appellate briefs and records?

A *brief* is your attorney's written argument of your position on the appeal. It sets forth the legal reasons why you believe *Briefs* that the lower court's decision should either be sustained or overturned. Considerable time is devoted by your attorney in researching prior cases, and the brief will contain those precedents in support of your position.

The *record on appeal* is a compilation of all the pertinent documents that went into the making of the decision that is being appealed. The record for an appeal of a pretrial order is far less substantial than one required for an appeal of a trial *Record on appeal* court's final determination. In the latter case, the record ordinarily includes the entire transcript of the trial—every question asked, each answer and everything else spoken "on the record." This can easily run hundreds of pages, and we have seen records that encompass several volumes. Reproduction costs in such instances may be highly prohibitive.

What goes into a retainer agreement?

Your retainer agreement should include all of the points discussed above, such as the fee and whether it is a flat or hourly rate, the responsibility for and definition of costs and disbursements and acknowledgment of the receipt of any monies paid *Contents of* by you as an initial retainer. The agreement should be in sim-*retainer* ple English, so that you can understand each of its provisions. *agreement* If you do not, question your attorney.

PHASE II:

DIVORCE

Chapter Five
LITIGATION TIME, OR SURVIVING A DIVORCE

A divorce action can mean prolonged emotional trauma. Even the lawyers do not always walk away unscathed. Part of the problem is that the parties rarely know what to expect or how long everything will take. Some are completely confused about what is going on, and the jargon and legalese used by many lawyers do not help matters any.

Court calendar congestion, pretrial discovery and motions and the unabated obstinacy of the parties result in delays that frustratingly fray the edges of anyone's patience. While this is true of any litigation, the effects are more pervasive and debilitating when issues such as custody, child support, alimony and property division are on the line.

HOW IT BEGINS

I understand that a divorce begins by personal service of a summons. What is meant by "personal service"?

Personal service simply means the personal delivery of the summons to the defendant. This is usually accomplished by someone handing the summons to your spouse. Who is authorized to deliver the summons varies from state to state. For example, in New York anyone over the age of eighteen who is not a party to the action may serve a summons. In other states, such as Florida, a deputy sheriff can do it. The purpose, however, remains the same everywhere: that of giving notice to the other spouse that a divorce action has been commenced.

Some states permit *substituted service* in lieu of personal de-

Personal service

Substituted service

livery. For example, the summons may instead be left with a person at your spouse's job and another copy mailed to him or her at home. Regardless of the manner by which service is accomplished, the person serving the summons must make an affidavit setting forth all of the facts of the delivery, which is then filed with the court. This is known as *proof of service,* and it is a requisite element of any divorce.

Proof of service

What exactly is a summons?

Gives notice and other information

A summons is a paper that gives notice of the divorce. It contains the names, and sometimes addresses, of the parties, the name and address of the plaintiff's attorney and the county and identity of the court in which the action is being commenced. Many states also require that the summons contain specific notice that the action is for a divorce. Printed summons forms are most commonly used by attorneys, such as the one illustrated below.

Sample summons

I think my wife has hired an attorney. Suppose I just refuse to accept the summons?

This reminds us of the classic story of the woman who, upon being confronted by a process server in the lobby of her building, held up her hands and screamed, "Get away from me, I am not touching that thing. You cannot make me take it."

Just to be on the safe side, she later called an attorney. Triumphantly she related how she had defeated her husband's efforts. When the lawyer stopped laughing, he told her that she better make an appointment because she had been served with the divorce papers, even though she had not touched them. He explained that the summons carries no magical powers that await the defendant's touch. The law is clear that it is sufficient that delivery be attempted and that the summons be left within the defendant's "zone of perception." After the process server had attempted to hand her the summons, it was good enough for him to have dropped it at her feet.

Zone of perception

In another instance, the process server was detected about a block away. The hapless husband ran into his car, which was parked nearby, locked the doors and started to drive off. The resourceful and agile process server leaped onto the hood and stuck the summons under the windshield wiper, like a parking ticket. Unfortunately for the husband, he treated the summons like a parking ticket. He ignored it. Service was later held to be

Supreme Court of the State of New York

County of New York

Index No.
Plaintiff designates
New York
County as the place of trial
The basis of the venue is
Residence of Parties

LISA R. ROBERTSON

Plaintiff

against

ARTHUR B. ROBERTSON

Defendant

Summons with Notice
Plaintiff resides at
110 Water Street
County of New York

ACTION FOR A DIVORCE

To: ARTHUR B. ROBERTSON, *Defendant*

You are hereby summoned *to appear or serve a notice of appearance, upon the Plaintiff's Attorney(s) within 20 days after the service of this summons, exclusive of the day of service or within 30 days after the service is complete if this summons is not personally delivered to you within the State of New York. In case of your failure to appear, judgment will be taken against you by default for the relief demanded below.*

Dated, September 2, 1982

Smith & Rogers
Attorney(s) for Plaintiff
467 Fourth Avenue
New York, N.Y.
212-678-9007

NOTICE: *The nature of this action is to dissolve the marriage between the parties, on the grounds*

of defendant's willful abandonment of plaintiff, as set forth in domestic relations law section 170(2)

The relief sought is a judgment of absolute divorce in favor of the plaintiff dissolving the marriage between the parties in this action. The nature of further relief demanded is:
  (a) suitable child support;
  (b) reasonable spousal maintenance;
  (c) proper distributive award;
  (d) equitable distribution of marital property;
  (e) sole and exclusive custody of the child of the marriage;
  (f) sole use and exclusive occupancy of the marital home; and
  (g) reasonable attorney's fees.

sufficient, and his lawyers were left with the task of opening the default divorce judgment against him.

What is an order of publication?

Suppose you seek a divorce, but your spouse cannot be found after several reasonably diligent attempts. You are even unsure whether he or she still resides in the state. For all you know, your spouse may be tending sheep in Australia. This does not mean that you must stay married. Under these circumstances, your attorney would then make an application for a court order permitting personal service by publication. This *Order of pub-* is what is meant by an *order of publication,* which will be *lication* granted upon a showing that your efforts have failed to reveal the location of your spouse.

The contents of the summons are published several times in one or more local newspapers. These are the legal notices that no one ever reads, being reproduced in small type and buried somewhere deep in the newspaper. Service of this type is ac- *Fictional ser-* tually a fiction. The odds are very remote that your spouse will *vice* see it. The practice dates from the time when communities were small and newspapers served as the only medium for information. Nevertheless, the U.S. Supreme Court continues to uphold the validity of such service, stating that it meets the *Meets mini-* very minimum requirements of giving "due notice" to a per- *mal require-* spective defendant. After all, the defendant's right to notice *ments* has to be counterbalanced against the plaintiff's right to start a legal proceeding, and a defendant cannot frustrate the latter's right by hiding.

I was present when my sister gave my husband the summons. Now he has apparently told his lawyer that he never got it. What can my attorney do under the circumstances?

Before your attorney can do anything, your husband has to *Jurisdiction* raise the defense of "lack of personal jurisdiction." This means *defense* that he claims he was never served and argues that the court has no business deciding the issues. Assuming that your husband makes this claim, your attorney would then proceed with what is called in most states a *traverse.* No matter what terminology is used, this is a short hearing confined solely to the issue of personal service. Your sister would be sworn as a witness, and she would testify about the circumstances surrounding the delivery of the summons to your husband. As you witnessed the event, you may also take the stand and testify. Your husband would then testify, as well as any witnesses that he *Court hearing* might be able to produce.

Usually, this would be an exercise in futility for your husband. It is a classic "Catch-22" situation. The judge usually *Catch-22* reasons that if your husband had enough notice of the proceeding to come into court to argue that he should not be there, the odds are pretty good that he had received notice of the divorce. Moreover, even if the judge decides that he was not served, your attorney will usually have someone stationed outside the courtroom to hand him another summons.

Now that the summons has been served, how long will it take for me to get my divorce?

This is really a question for your astrologer. Seriously, there are many variables that make it impossible to predict how long your divorce will take. First there is the complexity of the *Complexity of* issues involved. Are you arguing over ownership of the house, *case* or is it simply a matter of dividing the goldfish? Are children involved, and are custody and support problems evident? Is your spouse going to contest the divorce fully and attempt to prevent you from getting one? There are also external factors, such as case congestion in your local court. Sometimes even an undefended divorce must await months before it goes before a judge. As incredible as it may seem, in Manhattan Supreme, certainly one of the busiest courts in the country, there is only *Court calen-* one judge assigned to hear matrimonial pretrial motions. Con- *dar conges-* sequently, decisions often take months. *tion*

Another factor is the extent of discovery that must be conducted in determining the couple's assets and expenses. This varies from one case to another. Finally, there are obstinate delaying tactics and simple laziness. Some lawyers do not really move their cases that expeditiously, leaving matters *Other factors* lying in their files for months before doing anything. Other lawyers pride themselves in having the largest grab-bag of dilatory tactics this side of the Mason-Dixon Line, which they use to defend divorce actions and prolong them for years, hoping that you will relent out of frustration and settle for less.

There are two levels inherent in every divorce. First, there is the divorce itself, the dissolution of the marriage. In those few *First level:* states that still retain the fault concept, it is necessary to prove *dissolving* the other spouse's misconduct, such as adultery or cruelty. *marriage* Even in those states that have abolished fault, where it is only necessary to show irreconcilable differences or incompatibility, a divorce is not necessarily automatic. Your spouse may claim that the differences are not irreconcilable or that the parties are not incompatible; that everything is just fine and dandy.

The second level of divorce is composed of the economic and practical consequences. These include everything from the division of marital property to the custody of the children, as well as rights of visitation and obligations of support. As the emphasis has switched to considering marriage an economic partnership, this second level has received far greater attention. It is this level that will potentially cause the most delay in getting a divorce. Often, both spouses want the marriage to end, but they differ sharply on the terms. Until a settlement can be reached or a decision rendered by the court, a great many months will have passed.

Second level: economic and practical

The best way to survive a divorce is to adjust yourself to the concept of *litigation time*. Discard your normal references. Although you know that the divorce action will eventually get you from Point A to Point B, you must realize that your mode of travel may change. For example, it may ordinarily take you twelve minutes to get to the supermarket. You probably never stop to consider that this is because you go by car. Suppose you were to walk. Obviously you know the trip will take longer, and maybe you even figure that an hour should do it. So you begin your walk. It is a beautiful sunny day, and an hour in the fresh air does not seem all that bad. A few clouds begin to appear. Suddenly, the sky is darkly overcast, and it starts getting windy and cold. You wish you had worn a heavier jacket. Then comes the rain and thunder. You still have at least half an hour to go.

Adjust to litigation time

Picking up your pace, you slip and twist your ankle. Not only does it hurt, but you are now slowed by the injury. A truck speeds by through a puddle, drenching the few dry areas of your clothing. The rain finally stops, and your ankle begins to feel better. Then you run into Mrs. Greene, whom you have not seen in four months and who insists on catching you up with all the gossip. Finally, you disentangle and resume your journey. At long last, you see the store about three blocks away. You quell the temptation to run; there is still time left before closing. At least fortune has not totally deserted you. You begin your shopping, and you discover that the turkey that was on sale is sold out. The store manager offers to give you a raincheck. He says to come back tomorrow.

This story may seem silly, but we believe it illustrates the concept of litigation time. You may have an idea what will happen, but you do not know how long it will take. Expect delay, and be pleasantly relieved when there is none.

My attorney has informed me that my wife is "counterclaiming" against me for a divorce. What exactly is a counterclaim?

A *counterclaim* is just that—a countersuit whereby your Counterclaim wife, the defendant, asserts her own claims and allegations against you for divorce. Although she has the right to bring her own separate divorce action, her attorney, like most, has chosen to do it expediently in the form of a counterclaim. Actually, under most states' rules of civil procedure, your wife's counterclaim can be for anything; it need not be limited to divorce. However, as a practical matter, counterclaims in matrimonial actions are usually restricted to divorce-related claims. For example, you may have brought your action against your wife on grounds of cruelty. She counterclaims for a divorce against you based on irreconcilable differences, and she also includes another counterclaim for the return of her municipal bonds which are in your possession. The counterclaim will be included with her answer to your complaint.

What is an "answer" and a "complaint"?

The complaint and answer are what lawyers and the courts refer to as *pleadings*. Pleadings tell the story, plaintiff's side Pleadings (complaint) and defendant's side (answer). Their purpose is to define the issues and to give each party notice of those facts and circumstances underlying the divorce action.

Since you initiated the divorce action, you are henceforth called the *plaintiff*, or petitioner. Your wife becomes the *defendant*, or respondent. The labels vary from state to state; however, we will continue to use plaintiff and defendant for the sake of simplicity. At some point, your attorney will prepare and serve a *complaint* on your wife's attorney. The complaint Complaint sets forth certain facts, such as the date of your marriage, whether there are any children of the marriage and the important allegations concerning your grounds for divorce. If you seek a divorce based on cruelty, your complaint must contain specific allegations of your wife's misconduct.

Answer

Within a certain time provided by law, your wife's attorney must respond to the complaint by serving an *answer*. The purpose of the answer is to admit or deny the statements or allegations contained in your complaint. Those that are admitted are not at issue and do not have to be proven by you in court, e.g., the date of your marriage. Those that are denied by your wife become contested issues of fact that will require proof. If your wife decides to include a counterclaim, this will appear as a separate part of her answer. The counterclaim is essentially your wife's complaint, to which your attorney will have to respond by serving what is commonly called a *reply*.

Reply

Once an action for divorce is started, can I change my mind and drop the case?

Voluntary discontinuance permitted

Of course. No court will force you to get a divorce. If you change your mind because of reconciliation with your spouse, or for any other reason, you can discontinue your divorce action. The procedure differs, even in the same state. For example, in some states there is a specific time period during which you can discontinue the action unilaterally after which time you need the consent of the other party or a court order. The latter is extremely easy to obtain.

Does not affect spouse's counterclaim

Of course, if your spouse has counterclaimed against you for divorce, you cannot terminate his or her divorce action by ending yours. The counterclaim will still remain, and you will be forced to defend yourself against it. Often, a negotiated settlement of a divorce results in the plaintiff dropping his or her action and the defendant obtaining the divorce on the counterclaim, or vice versa. Or perhaps, after you have dropped your case, your spouse will, in turn, discontinue the counterclaim. But don't count on it.

DISCOVERING (AND DISCLOSING) ASSETS

One of the most important aspects of a divorce action is ascertaining the assets and income of both spouses. Only in this way can a court fashion a reasonable award of alimony, maintenance and child support that fully takes into account the needs of the dependent spouse and children as well as the other spouse's ability to pay, the factors that courts use in determining the actual dollar amount.

Why must I disclose my income to my wife's attorney?

Nearly every state has mandatory financial disclosure of one form or another. The purpose of such disclosure is to paint a picture of your net worth, which is defined as your assets and income minus liabilities. Only then can a court gain sufficient information with which to fashion suitable relief for the party demanding it. We have already seen that marriage is now widely treated as an economic partnership, so it is more important than ever that the assets of the partnership be fully disclosed. *Mandatory financial disclosure*

Certainly your income is an important factor for the court to consider. Many states have fashioned official *affidavits of net worth,* which require disclosure of relevant financial information such as bank accounts, short-term securities, stocks, bonds, partnership interests, life insurance, vehicles, real estate, salary, bonuses, commissions, dividends, interest, royalties, profit sharing, trust and pension benefits, fees, gambling awards and prizes, fringe benefits, inheritances and stock options, as well as your liabilities and expenses. *Affidavits of net worth*

Some of our clients are disturbed about the requirement that they disclose such information; however, there is nothing that can be done about it. A court can only make a reasoned decision if it is provided with all available information. Therefore you do not really have any choice. Your wife's attorney will get this information either the easy way or the hard way. If you refuse to disclose your income, he or she will make a motion to the court for an order compelling disclosure. Moreover, the court may award counsel fees that you will have to pay to her attorney on account of your needless intransigence. *Court can compel disclosure*

My lawyer sounds very confident that he will be able to discover my wife's net worth and demonstrate that she has even more sources of income than I do. He uses words like "interrogatories," "bills of particulars," and "EBTs." What is he talking about?

He is talking about the tools of discovery. Whenever financial issues are involved in a divorce, it is not uncommon to find one or both parties beginning to play games and trying to conceal assets. A husband with a reported weekly income of $400 and an unreported cash weekly supplement of $250 may very well experience short-term amnesia about the latter. Consequently, a conscientious attorney must make every effort to *Discovery devices: tools of the trade* discover all of a party's income and assets, thereby filling the marital pie. This is where discovery devices come into play. By the way, all discovery methods that we will be mentioning remain available to your wife's lawyer as well. When it comes to financial disclosure, both spouses are equally exposed.

Interrogatories require sworn answers

Interrogatories are written questions that your lawyer prepares and sends to your wife's attorney. Your wife must answer these questions in writing and under oath. In your situation, your interrogatories will attempt to elicit information regarding all the sources of your wife's income, bank accounts, stocks, dividends, bonuses, commissions and miscellaneous assets. She will also be asked questions about her employment and benefits, such as the free use of an automobile or travel allowances. Since your wife's answers are sworn, any contradiction between them and later testimony can prove devastating, impeaching (attacking) her credibility.

Bill of Particulars amplifies

A demand for a *bill of particulars* is similar to an interrogatory, but this device is restricted to statements or allegations made in the pleadings, i.e., the complaint or answer. The purpose of a bill of particulars is to amplify or expand upon those statements made in the pleadings. Thus, if the allegations in your wife's complaint are vague or ambiguous, your attorney can demand a more concise, detailed statement.

Examination before trial

An *EBT,* which stands for "examination before trial," or deposition, is one of the best ways of obtaining financial information from your spouse. Your attorney makes a demand for your wife's appearance, usually in his law office. A court reporter is present who stenographically or electronically records every word that is said during the proceeding. Your wife is sworn as if she were a witness in open court. Your attorney then asks your wife specific questions relating to her finances. Both questions and answers, as well as her attorney's objections, are recorded. It is just like "a dry run" for that aspect of the trial. The reporter later transcribes the examination into a bound transcript, which becomes the official record. We should point out that the procedure involves some expense. In some cities, the cost of the transcript is in excess of $2.50 per page, and we have seen transcripts running into several hundreds of pages.

Other useful devices

There are also some other discovery devices available to your attorney. One that is very useful is a *notice for discovery and inspection,* or *notice to produce,* as it is sometimes called.

This gives your attorney the right to require the production by your wife of certain specified documents and records, such as bank account statements, leases, employment contracts, stock brokerage accounts, and the like. Depending on the complexity of the records produced, your attorney may suggest that an accountant be hired to review them. Another discovery device that is sometimes important is a *notice* or *order for a medical examination.* This is appropriate where one spouse places his or her health in issue. For example, a husband may claim that while he is only forty-three years old, he has a debilitating heart condition that renders the likelihood of his continued employment doubtful. Consequently, the attorney may want to have a designated physician examine the husband and report independently.

Many of these discovery devices can be used on third parties, such as your wife's employer, her banker, stock broker, accountant and grandmother. Generally, your attorney must first demonstrate the necessity of conducting such non-party discovery. This is accomplished by setting forth those facts that give rise to a reasonable belief that such discovery is necessary. For example, your wife may reveal something in her interrogatories that requires further investigation. Discovery devices, when used intelligently and in tandem with one another, can be the most useful weapons in your attorney's arsenal, assuring proper pretrial preparation. *Discovery from third parties permitted*

Just how far can my wife's lawyer go in requesting disclosure of my income and assets?

The attorney can go as far as he or she needs, within reason. The purpose of discovery is to achieve the best picture possible of the financial history of the marriage as well as the present economic circumstances. Of course, the standard of reasonableness prevails in every state, and no attorney can conduct a fishing expedition or subject you to a medieval inquisition. *Reasonable limits*

The time and efforts devoted to discovery will vary in each case. For example, if you work for an hourly wage, have all your money in joint accounts with your wife, own an automobile on which the local bank has a lien and own a house on which the same bank has a mortgage, it is relatively easy to determine your net worth. The situation would be markedly different were you an individual who does not receive a regular paycheck. Suppose you are a hot-dog vendor, dealing in noth- *Discovery needed depends on your case* ing but cash. Here it may be necessary for your wife's attorney to obtain information from the suppliers of your franks, sauerkraut, onions and mustard in order to estimate the volume of your business. Or perhaps you are quite successful, having a multitude of investments, closed corporations and tax shelter schemes, which may only be fathomable by using independent accountants and auditors.

As can be seen, discovery is an important—if not the most important—aspect of divorce cases. The tentacles of discovery may probe into even the most inner sanctums of the parties' finances. However, the right is not unrestricted, and your lawyer may obtain a *protective order* from the court whenever the discovery demands become unduly burdensome and oppressive.

Before we went to the lawyers, my wife and I had already reached an agreement on how much alimony I would pay her. Now her lawyer is requesting that I produce all kinds of records and bankbooks. Am I being set up?

Disclosure necessary for informed decision

Not necessarily. A good lawyer will always request basic verification of your finances before permitting any agreement or settlement to be signed. Again, the lawyer's purpose is to assure that your wife is making an informed decision. Only then can her attorney advise her whether the settlement is reasonable or otherwise in her best interests. As a matter of fact, most separation agreements and divorce settlements contain standard language to this effect:

> Both the legal and practical effects of this agreement in each and every respect and the financial status of the parties have been fully disclosed and explained to each party. Both parties acknowledge that this is a fair agreement and is not the result of any fraud, duress, coercion, pressure or undue influence exercised by either party upon the other or by any other person or persons upon either.

This disclosure works as well to your advantage. In fact, do not be surprised if your own attorney volunteers verification of your finances. By making sure that your wife has access to relevant financial information, any later claim of fraud will be less likely to succeed. The integrity of the agreement or settlement is protected, and both parties can rest assured that their understanding will survive in the years ahead.

Okay, I can see the reason for some disclosure, but her lawyer is asking for copies of my tax returns for the past three years. I always thought that no one but the IRS gets to see a person's tax returns. Isn't this an infringement upon my privacy?

In a sense it is, but you should begin to realize that just about everything in a divorce action can be an infringement on your privacy. Not only will your personal finances be scrutinized, but if your divorce goes to trial, every other aspect of your marriage, including your fitness as a parent, may very well come out in testimony. This is certainly one of the more compelling reasons for most parties to settle their divorces before proceeding to trial. While tax returns are ordinarily considered private and not discoverable in civil litigation, the rule is just the opposite in matrimonial cases, since they are an important indication of marital property and income. Also, if you file joint returns, your wife can obtain copies of the tax returns directly from the IRS anyway. So there is little to gain by withholding your returns. *Tax returns discoverable in divorce actions*

By the way, if either one of you wishes to obtain copies of your joint tax returns for preceding years, all you need do is simply complete a Form 4506, pay the two-dollar fee and send the request to the IRS. These forms can be obtained at your local IRS office or from an accountant. *Obtaining copies of returns from IRS*

I have a safe deposit box with about $15,000 worth of jewelry inside. I never told my husband about the box, and now I'm wondering whether I should disclose the information or take a chance that no one will find out about it.

It may be an old saying, but it often does prove true that honesty is the best policy. Certainly this is something that you should discuss with your attorney, because the jewelry may be a crucial element of your financial posture.

Let's first see what this jewelry represents. Perhaps most of the jewelry came from relatives as gifts or by inheritance. You may have purchased some pieces before your marriage. This would constitute *separate property* that ordinarily would not be part of the marital pie for the court's division. On the other hand, your husband may have given you some of this jewelry, or you may have bought the items during your marriage. Then the jewelry would be deemed *marital property* and be subject to distribution in most states. Whether separate or marital, the *Separate or marital property?*

property is certainly an element of your net worth, and it must be considered by the court and your attorneys.

Deception can sometimes have unintended consequences. In

Unintended consequences

other words, it often backfires. A colleague once told us about a former client—we'll call her Mary Jane—whom he represented in a heavily litigated divorce. Her jewelry was actually worth over $60,000, but otherwise the circumstances were very similar to yours. Mary Jane had always concealed the existence of the jewelry from her husband, and she saw no reason why her lawyer should know about it either. She was sufficiently astute to realize that the less assets she showed, the more maintenance was possible.

At the trial, Mary Jane had survived two days of intensive cross-examination by her husband's lawyer. He seemed to be just about finished, and she was beginning to breathe a little easier and congratulate herself on a job well done. The existence of the jewelry had never come up. The lawyer interrupted his cross-examination and began rummaging through his briefcase, eventually pulling out a glossy eight-by-ten photograph. He had the court officer hand the photograph to Mary Jane, who recognized it as a picture that had appeared five years ago in the society column in the local newspaper. Her husband had been away for several months on an extended business trip, but this had not stopped Mary Jane from keeping her social calendar. In his absence, she had not been able to resist the opportunity to display some of her crown jewels.

The lawyer bore in on his prey, asking question after question about the jewelry. She first came up with the story that she had borrowed the gems from a friend, but she tripped over herself when it came to identifying the person. The lawyer was patient; he let Mary Jane supply her own rope. Mary Jane decided that the only thing that could now save her in the eyes of the judge was the complete truth. She admitted that she had a secret safe deposit box that was filled with jewelry.

Our colleague told us that the irony of the entire episode was that the jewelry had been inherited from Mary Jane's great-aunt. Therefore, it was not marital property and there had never been any risk that her husband would get any of it. Meanwhile, her unsuccessful cover-up destroyed much of her credibility, and our colleague feels that this, more than anything else, contributed to the unexpectedly meager marital award.

Since the divorce action was started, I heard that my husband is transferring all of his assets into his brother's name. When it comes to trial, won't my husband be able to plead poverty?

No. There are important safeguards built into every state's laws.

Parties to a divorce action must disclose all transfers within the past several years. Moreover, if your husband's brother received your husband's assets without paying a fair price for them, the transaction would be declared fraudulent, and your brother-in-law would be forced to return the property. The courts are extremely sensitive to any conduct that disturbs the financial status quo during the pendency of a divorce action.

Disclosure of recent trans-fers

Fraudulent transfers

Once again, discovery plays an important role. In your case, your attorney would be able to examine your brother-in-law to ascertain the circumstances surrounding the transfer of your husband's assets. There may also be document discovery, whereby all agreements, canceled checks and correspondence relating to the transfer must be produced for scrutiny. If the information elicited through discovery indicates that the transfers were fraudulent and an underhanded attempt by your husband to reduce his net worth, the court has the power to make the property distribution as if the transfer never occurred. Your brother-in-law will be ordered to turn a certain portion of the assets over to you. Your husband may have thought that he was being very original in his action, but there is not one judge who has not seen this before.

Discovery useful

An old story

If your husband has yet to transfer all of his assets, and you have a reasonable belief that he will be making fraudulent transfers, your attorney can make a pretrial motion seeking a court injunction to prevent your husband from transferring any marital property. This may even include the sale of his business. Generally, courts require a showing of a real and present likelihood of such transfers; mere supposition or fear will not suffice. Your attorney will be able to advise you whether you presently have grounds for the injunction. Your husband may have a legitimate business reason to transfer certain assets, which he would have to explain to the court. Certainly a judge will not attempt to unduly restrict his financial decisions, since they may have the effect of benefiting you as well.

Court injunc-tion against fraudulent transfers

My husband has always been involved in a cash business, and I know that much of his income is unreported. Is it possible to prove his true income?

Difficult to prove all income

It may be possible to prove a substantial portion of your husband's income, but if he is clever enough, some of it will never be discovered, notwithstanding the best attempts by your attorney. Unfortunately, this is a fact of divorce; an IRS auditor would certainly sympathize with you.

Circumstantial evidence

This is not to say that your attorney is prevented from using *circumstantial evidence.* He or she does not necessarily have to account for every penny your husband earned. Instead, a particular income level can be proven by examining the marital standard of living. For example, your husband may only report $125 a week and yet live in a $125,000 home and own three automobiles, a snowmobile, a motorboat and other luxuries. There are other less tangible indications of wealth, such as vacations, dining out, theater, country clubs and other forms of entertainment. Even the most clever practitioners of the so-called "underground economy" often trip up when it comes to enjoying the goodies of life.

Discovery of business practices

Discovery of your husband's business practices can also lead to important circumstantial evidence. For example, if he owns a retail clothing store, your attorney will want to know his suppliers. Perhaps their records will be subpoenaed to determine the amount of merchandise that your husband purchases each year. They also may be examined, either before or during trial, in an attempt to discover how many of the purchases were paid for in cash. Piece by piece, a picture of your husband's income may emerge. The focus may not be sharp, but the image will be recognizable.

Yes, but won't this discovery take forever?

Discovery takes time and money

It certainly will take a good deal of time for your attorney to conduct the necessary detailed discovery. It may also be expensive. This is as good a time as any to re-emphasize that the discovery stages of a divorce account for most of the delay in proceeding to trial. All your attorney can do is to proceed diligently in either making the discovery request, or by going to court when your husband or his attorney refuses to comply. This takes time. Some courts will not decide discovery motions for several months. Only you can judge whether the potential size of the marital pie warrants the time and expense of such discovery. However, do not be tempted to forego the discovery just because you want the divorce quickly. As we have seen, many an impatient spouse later regrets the rush to judgment.

The time you spend now in proper preparation can avoid years of agony and despair that will result from having to live with an unsatisfactory divorce settlement or decree.

From her very first meeting with her lawyers, Gail made it clear that all she wanted was "to get it over with as quickly as possible." She explained that she could not tolerate the situation any longer. Moreover, she and her husband had already *The case of* agreed to sell the house and divide the proceeds, along with *the impatient* their joint bank accounts, equally. As they were both teachers *spouse* making approximately the same salary, although employed in different school districts, Gail did not expect to receive any maintenance. However, her husband had agreed to continue paying the college tuition for Andy, their nineteen-year-old son.

Her attorney inquired as to other assets, but she replied that there would be nothing to find except the usual—two cars, household furnishings and the like. He then asked if she had copies of the parties' joint tax returns for the past several years. She said that she and her husband had always filed separate returns, something which she had in fact insisted upon from the beginning of the marriage. Her attorney then suggested that they first demand that her husband's attorneys produce copies of his tax returns as a safeguard, just in case there was something she had overlooked. A written request for the husband's tax returns for the prior five years went out that afternoon.

Some two weeks passed, and the husband's attorney finally replied that their client would not voluntarily turn over his personal income tax returns. Gail's attorney began to prepare a motion to the court for an order directing the husband to produce the returns. He explained to Gail that the procedure would take two or three months, assuming there was no appeal, but he was confident of ultimate success.

"Three months! Forget it—I can't wait that long," Gail said.

"Yes, but we don't have any choice. We need those returns." Her attorney tried to be patient. "Your husband may have additional sources of income that you're not aware of."

"That's impossible. There's no way he's smart enough to earn an extra dime," she snapped. "Besides, I've told you a thousand times that I want this thing over with. I want out of this marriage."

"As you wish, Gail, but I think you're making a terrible

mistake. Why don't you take another day to think about it and get back to me tomorrow?"

"Okay, but I doubt if I'll change my mind."

Gail telephoned her attorney the following day and reiterated her decision to forego the motion. She said she would take her chances. Her attorney once again attempted to persuade her to change her mind, but she remained adamant. Not even his follow-up letter, carefully setting forth the reasons for the discovery, convinced her. A settlement was reached a few weeks later, and Gail obtained her divorce shortly thereafter.

What Gail did not know was that her husband had been conducting a lucrative mail order business on the side for the past six years. The afternoons and evenings, as well as weekends, that she had assumed he was spending playing softball and drinking beer with the guys had been actually devoted to his thriving enterprise, the income from which he reported to the IRS as $60,000 per year. He had been leading a double life, with a studio apartment in the city and a Mercedes-Benz in the garage below.

Three years later, Gail was idly paging through an issue of *Forbes* in the dentist's waiting room, when in the "Up and Comers" section she was startled to find a short article on her ex and the recent multimillion-dollar sale of his business to an international conglomerate. Gail ran out of the waiting room still clutching the magazine, and drove straight to her attorney. The strenuous protestations of the receptionist went unheeded as Gail barged into her lawyer's office unannounced.

"Look at this," she shouted, throwing the open magazine on his desk. "That bastard is worth millions. And half of that is mine!"

Her lawyer hung up the phone and glanced at the article. "Not so fast, Gail. He's no longer your husband. Let me pull out the file and review this for a minute."

Gail could not contain her excitement as she watched him page through the documents and copies of correspondence in the file. "Well, what do you think?" she asked.

"I think what I thought three years ago. We should have gotten those tax returns," he answered.

"Tax returns—big deal. All I know is that the little sneak hid his business from me."

"That's exactly it. Had we looked at those tax returns, we would have been able to see that he was declaring income from the business, which I'm sure he had to. Then, with that clue, we could have obtained full disclosure, even if we had been forced to go to court for it. But Gail, I remember specifically that you did not want us to take the time to get those returns. You said that all you wanted was the divorce judgment as quickly as possible. As a matter of fact, here is a copy of the letter I sent you outlining the importance of pretrial discovery."

Gail looked at the letter. "So what does that have to do with anything?"

"What it has to do with," he explained, "is that your divorce is over—settled. You can't get anything from the sale of the business."

"That's ridiculous," she said. "He lied to me."

"Well, actually, he didn't, did he?" Her lawyer pointed out that nothing except her impatience had stopped them from getting proper financial disclosure before the settlement and that actually her husband had never misrepresented himself. He explained that this was not a fraudulent concealment; the business had always been there for everyone to see, if Gail had only taken the time to look for it.

Gail drove home in a daze. During the next week, she telephoned or interviewed about a dozen other lawyers. They all told her the same thing.

THE TRIAL

It all finally comes down to the trial. If the parties have been unable to reach an out-of-court settlement, the case must be tried. It is important to note that there are two elements involved. First, there is the aspect of the divorce itself. The party suing for a divorce must establish by credible evidence facts that will satisfy one or more grounds for divorce. These grounds vary from state to state, as does the degree of proof required for each. For example, in California proof of mere incompatibility is a sufficient ground for divorce. Some cases have even held that the very filing of a divorce action by itself establishes incompatibility. More traditional states, such as New York, take a much more hard-line approach. Incompatibility is not grounds for divorce in New York, which is a so-called "fault" state, requiring proof of abandonment, cruel and inhuman treatment, imprisonment or adultery before one can obtain a divorce that is not based upon a prior separation agreement. A chart appears in the appendix that lists the various grounds for divorce in every state.

The second element of a divorce action is the *collateral relief,* which includes property divisions, awards of alimony or maintenance, child custody, visitation rights and child support. As with the grounds for the divorce, the respective financial positions of both spouses must be proven in order to entitle either of them to any form of monetary relief. Similarly, if custody is disputed, each party will try to prove that he or she is the more fit parent with whom the children would be better off.

At the trial, evidence pertaining to both elements of the divorce action will be introduced, the credibility of the witnesses weighed and a final determination made. It is no wonder that the average person is extremely apprehensive about going to court.

What are the chances that our divorce will actually go to trial?

Most divorces settled out of court

Very slim. Over ninety percent of divorces are settled out of court. Nevertheless, when you retain an attorney, you must be absolutely prepared for the possibility, albeit remote, of going all the way. It is like the spare tire in your trunk; you hardly use it, but it is nice to know it is there. So it is with divorce. The better prepared you are for the possibility of trial, the better your chances of surviving the ordeal.

Impossible to predict

While it is impossible to predict whether your case will go to trial, you and your attorney should be able to get a sense fairly early on. If your spouse is unnecessarily recalcitrant and unable to compromise, if there are substantial money and assets at stake or if one party does not want the divorce, the probability of proceeding to trial is increased. It also depends on geography.

Logistical problems

If your court is in a densely populated county and has a heavy divorce trial calendar, which is not uncommon in the bedroom suburbs surrounding large cities, the inherent delay due to court congestion can mitigate against the decision to proceed to trial. Judges in such courts exert much more pressure on the parties to reach a settlement, because logistically there are just not enough courtrooms and judges to go around.

Avoiding trauma and saving money

Other factors make settlement attractive. The most important is the desire to avoid prolonged emotional trauma. A settlement offers faster resolution, control over the outcome, reduced exposure and greater privacy. On a practical level, it is also much less expensive. The more time an attorney must devote to your case, the higher the fee. Nothing consumes more time than a full-blown trial and the preparation for it.

How long does a divorce trial take?

Asking how long the trial will take is like asking us whether you will win. The answer obviously depends on all of the circumstances and facts of your particular case. Most divorce trials are completed in a few days. Others go on for months. If the grounds of the divorce are hotly contested or if there are many assets in dispute, the trial will take more time. Various *Length of* witnesses and experts may have to testify and reams of docu- *trials vary* ments will be placed into evidence. This is especially true if there is a family business. And if the issue of child custody is added to this equation, you can be sure that the court will be your second home for awhile.

There are external factors as well. A congested court calen- *Congested* dar may require the trial to proceed piecemeal—an afternoon *courts pro-* here, a morning there, the next session not until the following *mote delay* week. The attorneys may have other trial commitments that may require an adjournment and further delay. Witnesses may not be readily available. The judge may interrupt the trial and order a psychiatric evaluation of the children. Any number of unexpected "glitches" may crop up. We once had a client whose wife required hospitalization in the middle of a two-week trial. In that case a mistrial was declared, and the entire case had to be retried several months later.

What is a mistrial?

It is a trial that never happened. Even though there may have been weeks of testimony, some occurrence or technical defect requires the judge to declare a mistrial, voiding the entire proceeding. The parties must start all over again. It is like *Instant replay* drawing that card in Monopoly that reads "Go directly to jail, do not pass GO, do not collect $200." In our case, the delay occasioned by the other spouse's illness was too disruptive. The judge felt that the continuity of the trial had been broken, and that it would be fair to both parties to order a new trial after the wife's recovery. We are aware of one case where a husband grabbed his wife's attorney by the collar during his cross-examination in an uncontrolled burst of anger. The judge fined the husband but declared a mistrial, saying that he could no longer rule objectively on the wife's claim that the husband had previously assaulted her.

I've never seen a trial except on TV or in the movies, and I'm wondering what I should expect. Can you give me an overview?

Forget the movies and television. Any resemblance to the real thing is pure coincidence. Most divorce trials are tried without a jury, meaning that it is up to the judge to sift through the testimony and make the final determination. Conse-

Little chance for drama

quently, there is little opportunity for drama. The attorneys cannot play up to the jury with theatrical gestures designed to win their sympathy. Judges are too experienced for such tricks. Also, most of the testimony deals with the couple's finances, assets and property, the types of things that would get only an accountant excited.

The trial begins with brief opening statements by the two attorneys. These statements provide the judge with a road map of what issues will be presented. The plaintiff's side goes first. This usually means that the plaintiff takes the stand as the first witness in the trial, but this is not always the case. Sometimes if we are representing the plaintiff, we choose to call the defendant first, or other witnesses. This is a matter of tactics and strategy. The witnesses are first questioned by the plaintiff's

Examining the witnesses

attorney. This is called the *direct examination.* After he or she is finished with the witness, the defendant's attorney begins his or her *cross-examination.* If the cross-examination brings out any new matters or requires further elucidation, the plaintiff's lawyer has the opportunity of re-examining the witness; this is

Telling the story

called a *re-direct.* In such case, the defense has the right to a *re-cross.* This is how it goes, witness by witness, until the plaintiff concludes his or her case.

The defendant then has the opportunity to proceed. Sometimes a defendant's attorney will "rest" at this stage and put forth no testimony. However, it is much more common, at this juncture, for the defendant to begin to call his or her own witnesses. The procedure remains the same, except that the defendant's attorney conducts the direct, while the plaintiff's attorney now has the opportunity to cross-examine. At the conclusion of the trial, the attorneys may make a brief summa-

Don't expect instant ruling

tion, highlighting the positive points of their respective cases. Your biggest disappointment will probably come when, at the end of trial, the judge reserves decision. That dramatic moment of hearing the verdict is lost because judges rarely rule on divorces from the bench. Depending on the judge's workload, the decision will be forthcoming in a few weeks or even a few months.

The nature of the inquiry at trial is somewhat limited. Witnesses, for the most part, can only testify as to those things that they perceive with their senses, reporting on what they heard or saw. They cannot testify as to what they believe or what they feel; their opinions are of no moment. Therefore, do not expect *Opinions* that you or any witness will be able to use the courtroom as a *don't count* soapbox. The rules of evidence limit testimony to rather dry recitations of facts.

So much for the procedural and evidentiary side, which is fairly standard in any trial. The emotional aspects, on the other hand, are not so predictable. Divorce trials can become messy, especially if child custody is at issue. If you live in a state where *May be messy* marital fault is relevant in the determination of property awards, you must be prepared that your past conduct will receive close scrutiny. You may be asked embarrassing questions on cross-examination. Your testimony may relive incidents that you would have just as soon forgotten. Our only specific advice is to reveal everything to your lawyer, so that he or she can disclose negative details during the trial on your terms, or at least be prepared when they are gleefully brought out by the other side.

The divorce trial is about a week away. I'm literally scared to death. I'm afraid that even when I'm telling the truth I'll be so nervous that it will sound like I'm lying. Any words of advice before I enter the lion's den?

We are sure that your attorney will take the necessary time to prepare you properly before trial. This includes simulating some cross-examination. Once you get a feel for the type of questions that you will be asked, you will be more confident in providing the answers. Certainly you will be nervous, a normal reaction to a stressful situation. Judges realize that court is a *Practice* novel and disquieting experience for most, and they will take *makes perfect* this into account in viewing your credibility. In fact, most are rightly suspicious of witnesses who appear too cool and prepared. You will not lose your case because of a tremor in your voice. For the most part, it is what you say and not how you say it that counts. No Academy Awards are handed out at the end.

The best advice that we can offer is to insist that your attorney take time to prepare you properly for your ordeal. Usually, if there are are serious negative facts in your case, your lawyer will not leave it to his adversary to bring them out in cross-examination. Rather, he or she will make sure that the revelations are made during the more controlled circumstances of the direct examination. Even at this late date, make sure that your nervousness is not occasioned by your withholding from your attorney certain facts which you are afraid will come out for the first time at trial. Nothing is more devastating to the case than these tales of the unexpected.

Don't with-hold informa-tion

When you are on the witness stand, strive to answer only what is asked. Listen carefully to each question, do not anticipate and do not volunteer any information beyond that which the question requires. Try to relate the facts to the best of your memory. No one expects you to be a computer, able to reach into your memory bank and unerringly give the time, place and date of each and every occurrence. In the final analysis, preparation is the key to success—yours and your attorney's.

Responses should be short and to the point

Just before the trial started, the judge called the lawyers into his chambers, and after they came out about forty-five minutes later, my lawyer told me that the judge was putting pressure on him to settle the case. What is this "pressure" all about, and if I don't settle, will the judge hold it against me?

Lawyers, spouses and judges all have pressures prior to trial. For the judge there is the pressure of a congested trial calendar, not enough empty courtrooms and too many litigants. Settling a case takes much less time than trying one. Judges also feel that they have a duty to attempt to mediate a settlement between the parties, rather than allowing them to rush headlong into the trauma of a trial. Usually the judge is the first objective listener the parties encounter, and this objectivity often paves the way to a new slant on the issues that may result in a workable solution before the gavel is sounded. Thus it is not surprising that judges put some of their own pressure on attorneys to settle their cases.

Judges want settlements

The conferences in chambers are almost mini-trials. Each

lawyer has a chance to speak and present the best points of his or her case and the weaknesses of the opponent's. Sometimes documents and other proposed evidence are shown to the judge. Generally, the judge's reaction to the presentation is to make both sides feel that they have weak cases. Such an attitude will give any attorney cause to re-evaluate prior hard-line positions. One side may indeed be so weak or insubstantial *Re-evaluating* that the judge will give an indication of his likely ruling, *your case* telling the attorney that he better come up with more at the trial if he wishes to succeed. An attorney in this position, who knows exactly the cards in his or her hand, may be suddenly much more accommodating and willing to compromise.

Judges are also loath to see any litigant walk away from court with nothing. Even if they feel that a party has a weak case, they try to fashion some sort of relief. They point out to the attorney with the stronger case that paying something is better than risking all the marbles in a full-blown trial. Lawyers react differently to these pressures. Some buckle and waste *Pressures to* no time in throwing in the towel. A judge sitting behind his or *settle* her desk in the black robe can be very persuasive and formidable. Other attorneys are concerned that they will be appearing many times before the judge and do not wish to seem unnecessarily stubborn. Nevertheless, do not think that your lawyer's emphasis on settlement after such a conference means that he was bullied or turned by the judge.

The settlement conference gives lawyers a unique opportunity to glean an understanding of the judge's thinking. This insight can prove valuable, and your lawyer serves you well by *Obtaining ju-* recommending a settlement after such a conference. He or she *dicial insight* should be able to explain why the particular "package" or settlement is in your best interests, pointing out what little more there is to gain by going to trial and how much more there is to lose.

The judge's objectivity certainly plays a role. Remember, your lawyer is an advocate, a person who often identifies so strongly with your side of the case that he or she may become blinded to its weak spots or the merits of your spouse's case. By having had the judge put everything in perspective, your attorney may, for the first time, realize that some of your positions are indeed tenuous. Keep *your* perspective and listen carefully to your lawyer's suggestions.

*Reprogram-
ming your
thinking*

*How can my lawyer suddenly believe that some things about
my case are tenuous?*

The best way to explain this is to relate one settlement inci-
dent that occurred several years ago. The issue in that case was
custody. The children had remained with the mother during
the parties' separation, but now their father was seeking custody on the grounds that she was an unfit parent. The husband's main contention was that during the mother's absences
the children were left essentially unsupervised, since the thirteen-year-old was usually left in charge of the other three children. His attorney, a man whose own children were grown and
on their own, agreed with him that this did not appear to be
proper parental supervision. In chambers, the subject of custody was broached.

"Your Honor, we are prepared to prove," began the lawyer,
"that at least four times a week the mother is away from the
household during the early evenings and the only supervision
for the children is provided by the parties' thirteen-year-old
son."

"So what, counselor?" replied the judge. "Thirteen-year-
olds know a lot more than we used to when we were their age.
My daughter is fourteen, and she's been making some good
pocket money babysitting for the last two years."

"Yes, your Honor, but my client does not feel that the children are safe in the house when the mother is away."

"Well, do you have any evidence that the children are actually imperiled? Has there been a fire in the house?"

"No, but there is a possibility that something may happen."

"Oh, a possibility? Tell me, counselor, what arrangements
would your client make if he had the children?"

"Uh, he would try to get home earlier from work, and make
other arrangements."

"What other arrangements?" snapped the judge.

"I was going to say babysitters, but I get a sense that your
Honor may feel that the babysitters will be no older than the
thirteen-year-old boy."

"Exactly." The judge stood up. "Counselor, please go out
and talk to your client. It seems that this is the only issue preventing a settlement. Believe me, I will work closely with both
of you to work out the best visitation schedule possible for
your client."

A few minutes later, the lawyer found his client nervously

pacing the corridor. He explained what had transpired, and for the first time began to see for himself that his client's fears were a bit unfounded. He told the client that he believed that, under the circumstances, the judge would not be persuaded by their evidence and would most likely award custody to the mother. He recommended that the husband forego his claim and that the parties settle, since the wife's attorney had made several very reasonable offers on some of the other marital issues.

I've already missed three days of work because of waiting around court until a judge was free to hear our case. Are such delays common?

Unfortunately, yes. This is the fallout from the marked increase of divorces throughout the country, as well as other civil litigation. Moreover, many courts have transferred judges from civil to criminal cases in an attempt to keep stride with the rising crime rate. Many courts are overburdened and understaffed. There are only so many judges and courtrooms available. A judge also needs time to research and deliberate on cases that he or she has already tried, so not all of a judge's time is spent in the courtroom. Many judges detest trying divorces and will do almost anything to wriggle off matrimonial assignments. In Wiscasset, Maine, divorce cases are called in the county court only between 7 and 9 A.M., which reportedly has the profound effect of reducing trials and encouraging settlements. *Delays are common*

Delays unquestionably contribute to divorce settlements. It is amazing how, as the parties and their attorneys cool their heels for several days in the corridor, their heads also begin to cool.

Doesn't it just boil down to his word against mine at the trial?

For the most part, yes. There are generally two main witnesses in any divorce trial, the husband and wife. Not many people are around to witness the fight you had in the bedroom or one spouse's refusal to have sexual intercourse. However, as more and more states eliminate the fault concept for divorce, such testimony diminishes in importance. The real issues become the financial ones, and most of the evidence produced in this regard is in the form of documents, bankbooks, stock certificates and other tangible records. Moreover, there is increasing reliance on expert testimony, such as that of accountants or *Husband and wife, star witnesses* *Economic evidence: documentary* appraisers, upon whose testimony the final economic outcome often turns.

Even though each spouse will testify as to his or her expenses, such testimony is not taken at face value and it must be supported by corroborating evidence, such as bills, canceled checks and receipts. There are less accusations and finger-pointing in divorce trials nowadays, and sometimes it no longer matters whose version of essentially the same story the judge believes. The trend is to accept "the dead marriage" and concentrate on the resolution of the financial issues.

Testimony must be corroborated

Will I be able to speak to my lawyer during the trial?

Most certainly, but of course not when your lawyer is examining a witness or speaking to the judge. At all other times, you are free to consult and work with your lawyer. This is a constitutional right. Just try to whisper, not forgetting court decorum and rules of etiquette.

Free to consult

I have a best friend who has always been there when I needed her. Will she be allowed into the courtroom during the trial?

If your friend is not a potential witness for either you or your spouse, she will be permitted to sit through the entire trial, unless the court orders the courtroom cleared, which is rarely done. It is a policy of our law that all trials be conducted in the open. A judge will only prohibit spectators when the testimony is of such nature that the witness would be inhibited from testifying freely in the presence of strangers not directly connected to the case. For example, if a wife is about to testify that her husband forcibly sodomized her on several occasions, the rendition of the details in open court may be traumatic, inhibited and better done in a closed courtroom. However, spectators would only be excluded for that portion of the trial.

Court proceedings open to public

If your friend is a potential witness, most attorneys will demand that she be excluded prior to her testimony. Such demands are always granted. The reason should be obvious. If your friend has an opportunity to hear prior testimony, she will be in a position to confirm her testimony. Exclusion of potential witnesses minimizes the opportunity for collusion and deceit. Nevertheless, after your friend has testified, she will be free to sit as a spectator, provided that the other side has no intentions of their own to call her as a witness later on in the case.

Witnesses usually excluded

As a final note, even though your friend may be permitted to watch the proceedings, she must do it from one of the benches in the back. She cannot sit by your side, for that place is reserved for the parties and the attorneys.

I think my husband's boss would make a great witness for my case. But I doubt whether she will agree to come into court. My lawyer says not to worry, that all he has to do is "subpoena" her. What is a subpoena and how does it work?

A *subpoena* is derived from the Latin *sub poena*, which *Subpoena* means "under penalty." It is defined in *Black's Law Dictionary* (4th ed., West Publishing Company, 1968) as "a process to cause a witness to appear and give testimony, commanding him to lay aside all pretenses and excuses, and appear before a court or magistrate therein named at a time therein mentioned to testify for the party named under a penalty therein mentioned." In other words, whoever gets a subpoena has to go directly to court on the date set forth.

Your attorney, being an officer of the court, has the authority in most states to issue a subpoena. It is served just like a *Issuance and* summons, by personal delivery. It contains the name of the *contents* case and the party who is requiring the appearance of the witness, and it also sets forth that if the potential witness disregards the subpoena, a penalty will result.

What is this penalty? What happens if a subpoena is ignored?

Any person who ignores a subpoena can be held in contempt of court. The judge may issue a bench warrant for the forced *Contempt of* attendance of the witness. Moreover, the judge can fine or even *court* imprison the reluctant witness. Courts are not lax when it comes to the enforcement of subpoenas, because they are a necessary adjunct to the orderly prosecution of cases.

Often the subpoena will require the witness to bring certain records. A school teacher may be required to bring the child's school reports. An employer will be required to bring the payroll records. In most states, a small stipend must be given the witness by the party requiring the testimony, usually a few dollars for travel expenses.

During the lunch recess, I saw my wife's and my lawyer eating and joking together. All morning during the trial, they had been at each other's throats. What gives?

Sometimes it is difficult for clients to realize that their lawyers are only doing a job. How many times have you seen a

A job to do

prizefight where the pugilists attempt to knock the daylights out of each other, only to warmly embrace as the bell of the final round sounds? In baseball, Reggie Jackson always seems to be having an ongoing and friendly conversation with members of the opposing team, but this does not stop him from trying to hit every pitch out of the ballpark. Your attorney is a professional, and there is nothing wrong with him or her having a cordial relationship with a colleague. As one matrimonial lawyer likes to say, "My ire is for hire." What matters are the statements made in court—not in the cafeteria.

One last question: how do you think I'll do?

All we can do is relate to you an old adage in our profession that we tell our clients before trial: "Remember, it is never as good as you hope, but it is never as bad as you fear."

Chapter Six

WHAT DO I GET BESIDES AN EX-SPOUSE?

Courts have widespread, if not overwhelming, powers that for many years will affect the lives of divorced spouses. This chapter concerns the collateral relief, which can be as important as the dissolution of the marriage. The future rights and obligations of the parties, if any, must be carefully set forth in the divorce decree or settlement. The post-divorce relationship is created here, and the time and energy devoted at this stage to structuring a well-thought-out proposal can prevent many future problems.

PROPERTY DIVISIONS

There is increasing sociological and legal impetus to treat a marriage as an economic partnership. Instead of awarding alimony for life, many courts now are permitted to award maintenance payments for a specific period of time, coupled with a division of the couple's assets and property accumulated through the years of the marriage. Consequently, the subject of property divisions is becoming more important.

Who is going to get the house?
Before we can answer the question, we must elaborate on what you mean by "getting the house." A distinction must be drawn between residence and ownership. Regardless of the way your state treats marital property, your occupancy rights *Occupancy* may be at odds with your ownership rights. *vs. ownership*
For many families, the marital home not only represents a *rights*

roof over their heads but is their single largest asset and investment. Therefore, the ultimate determination of who owns the home is usually the most important property issue in any divorce action. Once each party's ownership interest is determined by the court or by settlement, the house is sold and the *Dividing pro-* proceeds divided between the parties accordingly. However, *ceeds from* there are times when, for a variety of reasons, the house cannot *house sale* be immediately sold.

One party may require occupancy of the home for a particular period of time. For example, when a court is confronted with a seventeen-year marriage with two children, one in his last year of high school and the other in eighth grade, a mother just getting back into the job market and a three-bedroom split level that the court has decided is owned equally, it will likely award the wife exclusive occupancy of the home for several years. The court's reasoning is based upon the following fac- *Temporary* tors: (1) minimal disruption for the children, who will be per- *post-divorce* mitted to remain in the familiar surroundings of their home for *occupancy* several years; (2) the wife's readjustment and entry into the job market in order to become self-sustaining; and (3) the husband's sufficient income enabling him to afford alternative suitable housing. Whenever there are young children involved, courts will try to maintain the home environment for at least a few years by awarding temporary post-divorce occupancy to the custodial parent. However, this is only feasible where the parties' financial circumstances permit such an arrangement. If one or both are in desperate need of the proceeds from a sale of the house, they will be directed to sell the home and share in the profits as specified by the court's ownership ruling.

When temporary occupancy is awarded in a divorce, there should also be a determination as to who pays the carrying charges on the home. This depends on the parties' respective fi- *Who pays the* nancial circumstances. If the non-custodial party has relatively *upkeep?* superior means, he or she may be ordered to incur these costs. Where their net worths are more equal, both may be called upon to share the expenses, or the parent living in the home may be made solely responsible.

The last issue that must be determined is the period during *Duration of* which the temporary occupancy will remain in effect. Gen- *occupancy de-* erally, temporary occupancy will be granted for a specific *pends on* number of years, but it will cease upon the first occurrence *many factors* of one or more of the following events: (1) the remarriage of the custodial parent; (2) the "emancipation" of the children, i.e., their reaching a certain age, moving from the home or becoming employed full time; and (3) the full-time employment of the custodial parent, perhaps at a specified annual income level. Of course, the parties can always by mutual agreement sell the marital home sooner. Finally, temporary occupancy is sometimes granted to a spouse even where there are no children; this may occur, for example, in the case of an elderly, financially dependent spouse with little prospects of gaining employment.

Temporary post-divorce occupancy is independent of ownership rights. We have seen a few cases where the husband was deemed to be the sole owner of the home, yet the wife and the children were nevertheless granted exclusive residency for many years. Ownership is determined according to your particular state's property and divorce laws. In equitable distribution states, many factors will be considered in determining the parties' respective ownership of the home, such as the length of the marriage, the financial contributions of the parties and other contributions such as homemaking services and the individual needs of each spouse, to name just a few. Not surprisingly, some of these factors are similar to those considered by the court in determining temporary pre-divorce occupancy. In community property states, there are few factors to consider since a presumption exists that a family home purchased during the marriage is owned equally by the parties. Finally, in title states, the name appearing on the deed signals ownership and, in most instances, controls. Practically speaking, most couples have an equal interest in the marital home in title states, because they are likely to have purchased the home in both their names.

Ownership determined: (1) equitable (2) community (3) title

As you can see, ownership is a determination made upon numerous factors. However, in our experience, if the marital residence represents the parties' main asset and it was purchased during the marriage, both parties will be awarded an ownership interest. It may not always be fifty-fifty, but courts do their best to come up with a fair and equitable arrangement when it comes to the question of who owns the home.

Usually divided fairly

Can a court order my husband to transfer the title of the station wagon to me?
Absolutely. The court's powers under your state's divorce

Delivering the goods

laws would be meaningless if it did not have the ability to require a spouse to transfer title to the other. Since title to an automobile is documentary in most states, it is necessary that your husband sign a transfer on the title and deliver it to you in order that you be able to enjoy exclusive ownership of the automobile. The same would apply to real estate or any other types of property that require documentary transfers. All other personal property is transferred by mere delivery. The court may have ordered you to turn over the antique liquor cabinet to your husband by a certain date. You do not have to sign anything; just make sure that the piece is available to him on the day agreed upon.

We both contributed equally toward the purchase of the $1,500 stereo unit. As part of the divorce judgment, the court decided that we are equal owners. So who gets the stereo? Do we get one speaker apiece?

Trading off

If you both think that this is the best solution, go ahead and divide the stereo, component by component. However, like most of us, you and your former spouse may rightly feel that half a stereo is useless, so you will have to make some other arrangement. Perhaps you can trade off your interest in the stereo for some other household items. Or one can purchase the other's interest at an agreed value. The last resort is to sell the stereo and divide the money equally. As you can see, the answer is more a question of temperament than of law.

My husband has always paid for his life insurance from our joint funds. Am I entitled to half of its present cash surrender value?

Life insurance may be marital property

In community property and equitable distribution states, a court can award you a portion of the insurance cash surrender value. The insurance is considered marital property because it was purchased during the marriage with marital funds. Consequently, it is an asset in which both parties have an interest. Only in community property states would your interest automatically be fifty percent. In equitable distribution states, your interest would be based upon a variety of factors. Your husband will usually be given a choice of either cashing in the policy and dividing the proceeds with you or paying you an amount equal to the cash surrender value.

The court's power is much more limited in title states, where it is most likely that you will have no interest in an insurance policy purchased solely in your husband's name. This holds true even if he bought it during the marriage.

For the sixteen years that we have been married, my wife has participated in her company's pension plan. Am I entitled to any portion of it once we get divorced?

Perhaps. If you live in an equitable distribution or community property state, the pension plan may be considered marital property in which you may be entitled to an interest.

Pension rights are very complex and still evolving, but we *Pension plan* can provide you with some basic guidelines. There are two im- *problems* portant concepts that must first be understood: whether your wife's rights in the pension plan have vested and whether they have matured. The terms are different and have distinct legal consequences.

Your wife's rights in the pension plan become vested after she has been employed for a particular length of time, which varies from plan to plan but is usually around ten years. A vested right is not forfeited if employment is terminated; it survives and benefits accrue. Only after rights have become vested can a pension be said to have matured, which means *Vested* vs. that after some additional time has elapsed, money can be *matured* withdrawn from the fund without penalty. Generally, pension *rights* rights mature upon retirement, death or termination of employment. The longer your wife remains employed with her company, the greater will be her ultimate benefits under the pension plan.

If your wife's rights in the pension plan have not yet vested, it will not be considered by the court. However, most community property and equitable distribution states hold that vested, *Only vested* even though unmatured, pension benefits constitute marital *plans become* property, which is subject to division between the spouses *marital prop-* upon divorce. A New Jersey court has held that such benefits *erty* are subject to distribution even though the enjoyment, i.e., maturity, may be postponed for many years.

In determining your interest in your wife's pension, the court will consider the length of your marriage, the duration of her employment and whether her pension benefits are vested. Another factor that will be considered is whether it is feasible to *Must wait for* give you a specified sum or some other property in lieu of a *payout* proportionate award of the retirement benefits. If you are given an interest in your wife's pension, the usual procedure requires that you wait until your wife collects her benefits before you get paid your share. Moreover, you will only be entitled to share in that portion of her benefits that are attributable to the years she was married to you.

The law in this area is in flux, however, and there are certain federal pensions that cannot be divided. The U.S. Supreme Court held in *McCarty* v. *McCarty* that federal law precludes a state court from dividing military retirement benefits. Many experts are waiting to see whether the Court will apply the same reasoning to private pensions that are governed under the Employee Retirement Investment Security Act (ERISA).

Some plans untouchable

What Social Security benefits are former spouses entitled to?
Before we answer the question, we must first distinguish the types of benefits available. The first category is *disability* and *retirement* benefits. The second is *survivor* benefits. Also, keep in mind that we are not talking about any benefits to which you are entitled because of your own employment, but rather benefits that are based upon your former spouse's employment history.

Disability and retirement benefits

In order to obtain either disability or retirement benefits, you must demonstrate to the Department of Social Security that you had been married for at least ten years prior to the divorce *and* that you are presently sixty-two years or over.

For survivor benefits, with some exceptions, you must show that you are presently unmarried, at least sixty years old and had been married for at least ten years prior to the divorce. You may be entitled to benefits ten years earlier, if you can establish that you are demonstratively disabled or that you have a child under the age of eighteen or that your child is disabled.

Survivor benefits

This is but an overview. The rules and regulations of the Department of Social Security are too complex to treat any more thoroughly, and we suggest that you contact your local office for more detailed explanations.

I have heard that some states allow a wife an ownership interest in a husband's business. Will this apply to my business, a business that I started over twenty years ago, before I even met my wife?
Sometimes a spouse may obtain such an interest. One of the most determinative factors is the length of your marriage. If you have only been married several months, your wife's claims will fall upon deaf ears. The longer you are married, however,

Awards of business interest

WHAT DO I GET BESIDES AN EX-SPOUSE? / 139

the more seriously her claims will be entertained, and under certain circumstances she may be awarded a portion of your ongoing business enterprise.

This award is not automatic. The court will first consider several specific situational elements. These include: (1) the income and property of each spouse at the time of marriage and at the time that the divorce action begins; (2) the duration of *Recognition* the marriage and the parties' ages and health; (3) the liquidity *of direct and* of all marital property; (4) the probable future financial cir- *indirect con-* cumstances and earning potential of each spouse; (5) the feasi- *tributions* bility of creating an interest in any ongoing business, corporation or profession; and (6) any direct or indirect contributions made to the business by the other spouse, which include joint efforts or expenditures as well as contributions and services as a spouse, parent, wage earner and homemaker. The last element bears closer examination.

There is an increasing recognition today of the economic impact of a spouse's homemaking services. In your case, your wife may have maintained your household and raised the children during the fifteen years that you were married. Her efforts *Homemaking* certainly freed you from these responsibilities, so that you *services as* could devote more time and energy to the growth of your busi- *major consid-* ness. Moreover, your wife may have helped entertain clients or *eration* customers, as well as prospects. She may have accompanied you on a number of business trips for such purposes or come into the office several times to pitch in with the year-end bookkeeping. Perhaps she even allowed you to take all of the money from the wedding gifts—half of which was rightly hers—and invest it in the business. Finally, just her emotional support during those hard times encountered along the way may be viewed as a legitimate contribution toward your success. Your wife will be permitted at trial to testify as to all of these ele- *Emotional* ments, and a court, in its discretion, will be allowed in a com- *support is fac-* munity property or equitable distribution state to award her a *tor* specific interest in your business.

Suppose the court gives my wife twenty-five percent of the business. Does that mean that she is entitled to move into the office next door to me?

No. A court will make sure that your divorce is really a divorce, and it will not plant the seeds of a new business relationship by giving your wife a seat on the board of directors.

Cashing in on interest

The judge will direct that your wife "cash in" on her interest in a variety of ways. There may be a long-term payout, based upon the value of that twenty-five percent interest at the time that the divorce action started. It may be more feasible for you to give your wife a single lump-sum payment. On the other hand, your wife may continue to enjoy twenty-five percent of the profits of the business for a set number of years, as determined by the court. In some instances, this profit-sharing continues as long as the business does.

My husband and I started our publishing company together when we were first married nine years ago. For the first five years, we worked together side by side, and many of my ideas were adopted and proved successful. Then our oldest was born, and I stopped working. Meanwhile, I had always assumed that I was an equal owner, but now my husband tells me that all the stock is in his name. What will the judge do?

Direct contributions by spouse

This is an illustration of a wife's direct, as opposed to indirect, contributions to the family business. You will be permitted to testify at the trial as to all of your efforts. Witnesses, such as employees or customers, may be used. Sometimes documentary evidence may be introduced, such as business records in your own handwriting or correspondence. Moreover, your work at the beginning of the enterprise will be viewed very favorably; courts recognize that the initial energy and time devoted to the creation of a business is often more arduous and crucial than time devoted to the maintenance of the business after it has already been established. Your goal is to demonstrate efforts directed to the growth of the business. And don't forget about these four years of child-rearing; as we explained in the preceding answer, this indirect contribution will also be considered by the judge.

Court may okay an active role

Taking everything together, it is quite likely that you will be awarded a substantial portion of the publishing company. The court is not bound by the fact that your name does not appear on any of the stock certificates, and it can order the corporate records to be amended to reflect your true ownership. Finally, since your past contributions were so direct, the court may in your case order that you be permitted to take an active role in the management of the business if you so desire. Good luck, partner.

I started my business right after we were married, but my wife has always had her own career. True, she is the mother of our children, but we have always shared the domestic chores pretty equally. Now her lawyer is making noise about her getting a piece of my business, saying that she helped entertain clients. Where do I stand?

You should have nothing to worry about. Under these circumstances, your wife has no legitimate claim to a proportionate share of your business. Certainly much of her time has been devoted to her own career. Her so-called indirect efforts to the family and household seem to have been matched by yours. Taken alone, entertaining clients is hardly a peg strong enough to hang an equitable distribution claim on. *Little to be worried about*

Allowing one spouse to have an interest in the other's business is really extraordinary, and a court will grant it infrequently. The court usually will look for other ways to reach a fair result, such as increased maintenance or a larger share of other marital property. However, in some cases, an award of a business interest is necessary to compensate a spouse adequately for his or her services through the marriage. Yours does not seem to be such a case, since your wife will be left with her own career and is not financially dependent upon you. *Proportionate share of business is unique and rare relief*

Here is my situation: we got married just before my husband began medical school. I worked as a legal secretary to support us during the seven years it took him to become a surgeon. Two years have gone by, and he has his own practice, drives a Mercedes-Benz and, as I just found out, he is paying upkeep on two apartments—ours and his girlfriend's. He tells me that he wants a divorce, and I am wondering whether my past sacrifices will be considered by a court so that I can get a portion of his future earnings as a physician.

Divorce courts are beginning to encounter what Judge Krafte in New Jersey has called "the medical school syndrome," of which your case is a vivid example. The question that you present is whether a professional school education and medical license acquired during the marriage is "marital property" subject to equitable distribution. Unfortunately, although we can define your question, we cannot be very precise with our answer. The states are divided over this issue, and they approach the problem in varied ways. *States are divided over professional license issue*

*Assets vs.
earning ca-
pacity*

*What's it
worth?*

*Restitution
(pay-back)
and enhanced
earning ca-
pacity*

*A decision
against the
tide*

*License may
be marital
asset*

If you assume for a moment that the medical degree is an asset, you must realize that the value of that asset is distinct from your husband's ability to use it and develop his own earning capacity. His earning capacity will vary according to his own talent and other external circumstances. The thorniest issue has been placing a dollar value on the medical license; it is not something that can be sold in the open market like a liquor store license. California has refused to treat a professional license as community property for that reason. Many equitable distribution states, such as New York, Indiana, Colorado, Iowa and Oklahoma, have also refused to grant a spouse an interest in a professional license; other states, such as Ohio, Michigan, Kentucky and Minnesota, will make an award that is really based upon *restitution,* i.e., paying the supporting spouse back for the money expended for tuition and the like. Although refusing to treat the medical license as an asset, some of these states will consider the enhanced earning capacity that it confers on the other spouse in their award of maintenance or other equitable distribution.

A noted and controversial exception to the general rule is Judge Krafte's decision in New Jersey on December 5, 1980, in *Robert Lynn* v. *Bonnie Lynn.* The learned judge determined that the medical degree was indeed a marital asset subject to equitable distribution. He rejected the traditional view that a professional license, because it cannot be sold like a commodity, is not property. Nor was he persuaded by the argument that it has no value to any person other than the holder, that it is nothing but an indicia of achievement and a legal authorization to practice. The judge refused to foreclose the possibility of sharing merely because many may believe that the pursuit of a professional degree is really an individual effort, that it is the person obtaining the degree who must study, learn and pass examinations in order to acquire it. Judge Krafte made a veritable call to arms, stating that "we should not be hesitant to light the torch and probe into the darkest recesses of this syndrome in order to equitably illuminate the injustices which strict adherence to traditionalist concepts would otherwise require." He pointed out that just because it is "difficult" to determine the value of a particular asset does not mean that a court can sidestep its responsibility. This decision is now being appealed by the husband, and some of the other states mentioned have not yet had rulings from their highest courts. The waters remain *Still in flux* uncharted.

ALIMONY AND MAINTENANCE

In marriages of long duration, alimony and maintenance orders are to be expected regardless of the extent of property divisions, unless both spouses have been gainfully employed and have approximately equal income. *Alimony* is the traditional form of relief; it usually lasts until the dependent spouse either dies or remarries. With the advent of community property and equitable distribution laws, the concept of maintenance has emerged. *Maintenance* payments are temporary, usually for a specified duration, and they are designed to enable the economically dependent spouse to become financially independent. The payments are usually designed to last until the person can acquire sufficient educational or vocational training to enter the work force. The amount of maintenance usually depends upon the person's needs and the extent of the property and assets that were divided between the spouses.

It is a sad commentary on our laws, and perhaps society itself, that many financially dependent spouses never receive the maintenance (and child support) payments to which they are entitled. Post-divorce enforcement proceedings are in the main cumbersome and unreliable, and, if the providing spouse is adept at concealing himself, his assets or his income, there is not much anyone will be able to do about it. For this reason, we recommend to many clients, where the situation permits, to maximize on the property share even if it means trading off some maintenance. It is better to get now than expect later. Naturally, not every marriage has sufficient property and assets to permit such negotiating, and for many there is no alternative but to rely on a reasonably adequate maintenance award.

How does a judge decide how much alimony or maintenance should be paid?

In awarding spousal support, be it alimony or maintenance, most courts consider the following factors—in fact, some are *Factors con-* required by law to consider them: the parties' respective in- *sidered in* comes and marital property; the length of the marriage; the *maintenance* ages and health of both parties; the present and potential earn- *determina-* ing capacity of both; the time period and training necessary *tions* to enable the person with the financial needs to become self-supporting or enter the job market; the presence of children and their ages; the preseparation standard of living; the various inheritance and tax consequences; the dependent spouse's homemaking contributions and services, if any; and any other factors which the court deems important and relevant. In some states, this last consideration can encompass the underlying reasons for the divorce, i.e., who is to blame for the breakup.

What do you mean by that last statement?

Some states permit a judge to take into account marital misconduct in awarding alimony or maintenance. A financially dependent spouse, who the court finds committed such acts as adultery, cruelty, abandonment or other such conduct, may be awarded less maintenance and property than he or she would otherwise have been entitled to. On the other hand, the more financially able spouse who is found guilty of such marital misconduct may get less property and higher or longer maintenance obligations. Although maintenance is not supposed to be a punishment, courts get around this and justify higher awards by finding that the misconduct caused serious distress to the dependent spouse that will likely inhibit or prolong his or her adjustment. This is true even in some states that have abolished the traditional fault grounds for divorce where, though a party need not show fault in order to get a divorce, such evidence may be introduced for the judge's consideration when it comes to determining maintenance and property division.

Misconduct by spouse may affect maintenance and property division

The following states provide that any marital fault responsible for the breakdown of the marriage may be considered by the court in determining property disposition and maintenance awards:

States that can consider marital fault

Alabama	Michigan
Connecticut	Missouri
Florida	New Jersey
Georgia	New York
Hawaii	North Carolina
Idaho	Rhode Island
Indiana	South Carolina
Maryland	South Dakota
Massachusetts	Tennessee
Texas	

The following states exclude consideration of fault in determining maintenance and property awards:

Arizona	Kentucky	
Colorado	Minnesota	*Those that*
Delaware	Montana	*cannot*
Illinois	Pennsylvania	
	Washington	

Interestingly, Illinois and Pennsylvania retain fault grounds for divorce, yet refuse to take marital fault into consideration when determining maintenance and property awards.

I've heard that the shorter the duration of the marriage, the less amount of maintenance the spouse has to pay. Is this true?

Yes. The duration of the marriage is a major factor in maintenance considerations. However, as we have pointed out, there are many other factors that the court will consider. *Length of marriage a factor . . .*

The circumstances of each divorce are different. The fact that you have a friend who was married the same length of time as you does not mean that you will be paying the same amount of maintenance as he. Your income, your family's needs, your marital assets and your wife's and the children's ages may indeed be different and result in a greater or lesser award. Finally, no two judges are alike. They each bring their own set of values and prejudices to the bench; the gavel and robe do not come with an electronic maintenance calculator. *. . . but not the only one*

I read recently that a husband received alimony from his wife. Is this some kind of a new trend?

This trend has been developing in many states over the last fifteen years. The process was quickly accelerated, however, by the U.S. Supreme Court on March 5, 1979, when it handed down the *Orr* v. *Orr* decision that requires all states to make their spousal support laws gender-neutral. Courts now inquire as to the respective needs of the parties, not their sex. *Gender-neutral*

What is meant by preseparation standard of living?

This is the standard of living that the couple enjoyed prior to the divorce action. This includes the home you lived in, the car you drove, the clothes you wore, the vacations you took, the restaurants you dined at, the clubs you joined, the private schools or colleges that your children attended and the disposable income you enjoyed. And a number of other things we probably left out, but you get the idea. *Prior lifestyle*

Indication of net worth

The preseparation standard of living is a good indication of the couple's net worth and is used as one of the guidelines in deciding maintenance. By the same token, courts are cognizant that divorcing couples must make adjustments, since it is impossible for them to maintain the same standard of living after they separate.

My husband argues that I shouldn't get any support from him because I could get a job. Although it is true that I have a marketing degree, it was my husband who always told me that he didn't want a wife who worked. Now, having been out of the job market for fifteen years, I am finding it extremely difficult to find one. Do my husband's arguments have any validity?

Re-entry problems considered

We sympathize with your predicament, and so will a judge. You have been out of the job market for fifteen years, and presumably you have depended upon your husband's income during that time. No one expects you to obtain employment that suddenly replaces your husband's financial obligations. Even with your best efforts a job will not come easily, for you lack requisite experience. You will also be competing with much younger individuals. It will take you some time before you are gainfully employed. Perhaps you will be forced to take something outside of your field or a low-paying, entry-level position until the proper opportunity presents itself.

Financial rehabilitation

Courts take this all into consideration. The modern concept of maintenance is rehabilitative. A judge will structure an award that will attempt to provide you with sufficient income until you get back on your own two feet. This does not mean, of course, that you get a free ride. The fact that you have a college degree affects your earning potential, which will be taken into account by the court in fixing the amount and duration of your maintenance.

How can a judge possibly determine my "earning potential"?

Comparable evaluation

No judge can define your earning potential with any degree of certainty; it is an elusive concept. Nevertheless, it is possible to take into account your prior training, experience, age and health, and match those factors to someone with similar statistics employed within your geographical area. Perhaps your husband's attorney will produce an expert witness to testify at trial about the job opportunities available. You would then be permitted to show that such testimony is not applicable to your case. For example, you may have young children at home requiring your full-time personal supervision and making it impossible to be employed full-time.

I don't mind paying support to my wife . . . until she finds a job. Does a judge have the power to order that maintenance payments be stopped once she is employed?

Yes. Maintenance is generally fixed for a specific period of time, which usually is a fair estimation of the time that it will *Time limits* take for the financially dependent spouse to become self-supporting. Some awards or settlements, however, have built-in provisions that the maintenance payments will cease upon the wife's employment. Frequently, employment must be for a specified salary, so as not to discourage or penalize the wife who takes a low-paying, entry-level job.

I got a great deal on my house about seventeen years ago, which was two years before we got married. With the crazy real estate market the way it is, I was shocked to learn that it is now worth about a quarter of a million dollars. I wish my salary had gone up as much, for it has continued to be rather modest, and I have no other source of income. In determining my maintenance obligations, will the judge take me to be worth $250,000, and if so, won't I be forced to sell the house to enable me to make good on the payments?

Your net worth is an important factor in determining maintenance awards to your wife. You are holding a valuable asset, *Important* and a judge will not ignore it. The ultimate resolution turns on *asset* whether the house is marital property.

At first glance, the house appears to be separate property, since you bought it well before the marriage. However, we assume that you did not pay for the house entirely in cash. Rather, like most individuals, you took out a long-term mortgage and made the mortgage payments during the marriage with marital funds. Consequently, your wife can claim that she *Is it separate* is entitled to an interest in the house. For example, say that you *or marital* purchased the house for $20,000, placing $10,000 down. The *property?* remaining $10,000 was financed by a fifteen-year mortgage, which was paid off during the marriage. One half of the purchase price was thus paid with marital funds. Your wife may then claim that she is entitled to a share of that and one half of the house's appreciation. She may also be able to point out certain improvements that were made to the house during the marriage which were paid for with marital funds and which enhanced its value.

Counter-argu-ment

A counter-argument is that separate property means just that, and because you bought the house before the marriage, it must be excluded from the marital pie. It can be said that your wife had the benefit of living in the home all these years. The marital funds used to pay the mortgage would have had to go for rent had you not purchased a house before the marriage. Your wife cannot now take advantage of your business acumen.

Both arguments have equal validity, and the answer has gone either way in cases that we have reviewed. The outcome is important because the division of marital property has a direct effect on maintenance awards. If the judge finds the first argument persuasive, your wife will be given a financial interest in the home, which in all likelihood would reduce your monthly maintenance payments. On the other hand, if the judge buys the second argument, you get to keep the house, but your maintenance payments will undoubtedly be higher, since your wife will not be able to rely on the house money. Looks like you lose either way.

Will not be forced to sell separate property

Assuming you get to keep the house, a court will not require you to sell it in order to meet your maintenance obligation. However, on a practical level, you may find that you have to take out a second mortgage or tighten your belt a bit.

CUSTODY, VISITATION AND CHILD SUPPORT

If there are minor children, the divorce decree or settlement will specify either joint custody or which parent is to receive permanent custody. It will also set forth the amount of child support, if any, that the non-custodial parent will pay periodically, along with any other such obligations that are permitted under state law or agreed upon by the parties. Finally, the specific visitation rights of the non-custodial parent may be included, although many lawyers and judges are satisfied to state merely that there are to be "liberal visitation rights."

I've heard that there is a presumption that children should be with their mother. Do women have an advantage when custody is at issue?

Legally, no; psychologically, yes. Most states by law have eliminated a presumption in favor of either parent. This is an *Law favors* important change from earlier times when the mother was pre- *neither spouse* sumed better equipped to raise the children, and the law required that the father first demonstrate the mother's unfitness before his application for custody could be entertained. Society and the law have come a long way since then. Today, even with custody battles involving children born out of wedlock, there is no longer an automatic legal presumption in favor of the mother.

What the law says, however, can differ from what it does. The elimination of the presumption in favor of the mother did not wholly succeed in overcoming the deep-rooted judicial disposition that children should be raised by a female. Most *Traditional* judges come from a time when it was rare for both parents to *attitudes pre-* participate in child-rearing duties. More likely than not, the *vail* parental roles in their families were traditional, with the father working and the mother staying home to raise the children. Consequently, many judges find it difficult to justify awarding custody to the father, unless the mother is demonstratively unfit as a parent.

Attitudes are changing. As many fathers begin to reverse the traditional roles and assume greater child-rearing responsibilities, judges are becoming more comfortable with the notion *More fathers* that males are fully capable of raising children. As a result, *are obtaining* both parents now come to court on a more equal footing. *custody* Courts place more emphasis on the child's best interests than ever before, and the number of fathers obtaining legal custody of their children increases each year.

Is there a difference between legal and physical custody?

Yes. Until there is a formal determination by the court or an agreement by the parties, both parents have *legal* custody of *Equal input* the children. This means that each parent has an equal say in *... equal pos-* the decisions affecting their education, medical care, welfare *session* and upbringing. *Physical* custody refers to the actual possession of the children at any given time. Assuming the parties have separated, one parent will usually have physical custody of the children.

Will I still have a say in major decisions affecting the well-being of the kids, such as schooling, if my wife is awarded custody?

Non-custodial parent loses authority

Once the parties (by agreement) or the judge (by decree) determines which parent is to have custody, the non-custodial parent usually loses the authority to make the day-to-day decisions regarding the children's welfare and upbringing. This does not mean that the parties cannot agree to a different arrangement.

Agreement for continued input in major decisions

Many divorce settlements and separation agreements awarding custody to one parent also contain a provision that the non-custodial parent will continue to take an active part in making major decisions affecting the children, such as those concerning education and medical care. However, if your agreement or divorce decree is silent in this regard, it is unlikely that you will have an equal say in such matters, unless your wife is willing to confer with you and respect your views. We always encourage our clients to participate as much as possible in the decision-making process, because we feel that mutual parental input is always in the best interests of the children.

What is joint custody?

Sharing decisions

Shared physical custody (optional)

Joint custody is an arrangment whereby both parents maintain legal custody of the children. This means that both parents must confer with one another on all major child-rearing decisions. Neither parent's say is greater than the other's. Many joint custody arrangements also provide for *shared* physical custody. The time spent with one parent is as equal as possible to the time spent with the other parent. We know of one case in New York City where the children stay where they are and the parents alternate between two separate residences. Obviously, shared physical custody arrangements often prove impractical unless the parents live in close proximity and maintain a cooperative relationship.

Sometimes difficult

Shared physical custody is difficult to maintain, and many parents who begin such an arrangement soon discard it as overburdensome and unwieldly for all concerned. They soon discover that the essence of joint custody is the mutual control over the children's welfare and not the actual time spent with them. Many parents are thus willing to forsake shared physical custody as long as they maintain this control and continue to enjoy free and easy access to the children.

Today a number of states, such as Michigan, require by law that joint custody be awarded unless circumstances dictate

otherwise. In other words, there is a presumption that there
should be a joint custody arrangement, at least as it relates to
parental input. The judge can still make one parent the physi- *New legisla-*
cal custodian of the children for most of the time. Legislation is *tion*
pending in many states to create this same presumption in
favor of joint custody.

What is split custody?

Split custody refers to a situation where the children are divided between the parents. For example, seventeen-year-old *Separating*
Tommy may go with his father, and nine-year-old Cindy with *children very*
her mother. Such arrangements are rare and usually frowned *rare*
upon, and you do not have to be a psychologist to understand
why. The parents' divorce is traumatic enough without adding
to that a sibling separation. There are instances, however,
when such an arrangement proves to be in the best interests of
the children. This will usually occur where there is an appre-
ciable difference in their ages and each articulates a preference
for such custody arrangements. In such situations, the court
feels that the age difference reduces the hazards inherent in
awarding split custody, because in reality the children did not
"grow up" together. Still, there have to be other persuasive and
extenuating circumstances.

*What type of visitation arrangement is best for me and the
children?*

While it is of course impossible to specify categorically the
ideal visitation arrangement, since it depends so much upon
the needs of the children and the schedules and availability of
the parents, some general observations can be made.

Flexibility is the key, and the parents should try to develop *Flexibility is*
informal responses to changing circumstances and needs. *the key*
However, it is vital that the ground rules be set—in detail. In
this way, if problems should later develop regarding visitation
rights, there is a readily referable basis from which a judge can
determine the parties' rights. Therefore, be sure that the visita- *Set ground*
tion schedule is specific about occasions such as holidays and *rules*
birthdays, and even that it defines what is meant by "a weekend." A typical, detailed visitation provision would look like
this:

> The mother shall have absolute custody of the parties' two
> children during their minority, and she is granted exclusive *Sample clause*
> supervision, control and care of them, such absolute custody

subject, however, to the rights of the father, as hereinafter set forth:

(a) The father shall have the right to have the children with him every other weekend. For purposes of this agreement, a weekend shall be deemed to commence at 6 P.M. Friday and to end at 7 P.M. Sunday. The mother shall make the children available at her residence so that the father may pick up the children at said residence, and the father shall return the children to the mother's home at the end of his visitation period. If the father cannot take the children on any particular weekend, he shall give the mother forty-eight (48) hours' prior notice thereof. In such event, he shall not, without the mother's consent, take the children on the following succeeding weekend but shall wait until the next following alternate weekend.

(b) The father shall have the right to visit with the children one day during the business week, on Tuesday of said week. He shall have the right to take the children from the mother's home during said evening visitation, but in no event shall return the children to the mother's residence any later than 10 P.M. In the event that the father is unable to visit the children on Tuesday evening as set forth herein, he shall give the mother twenty-four (24) hours' prior notice of same and shall have the right to visit on another evening of that week so long as it does not unduly interfere with the mother's and/or the children's schedule.

(c) The father shall have the right to have the children with him on the following holidays, in alternate manner:

New Year's Day	Lincoln's Birthday
Washington's Birthday	Easter Sunday
Memorial Day	July Fourth
Labor Day	Thanksgiving Day
	Christmas Day

(d) The father, after prior consultation with the mother, shall have the right to be with the children on the children's birthdays each year, for one half (½) of the day.

(e) The father shall have the right to have the children with him for a total of four consecutive weeks each summer period; "summer period" being defined as the period being from on or about June 25th to on or about September 7th. The father shall give the mother at least sixty (60) days' prior notice of his election to take the children for his summer visitation. It is understood by the parties that the father may have legitimate business commitments which make impossible or impracticable the keeping of the entire summer visitation schedule subsequent to the father's notification as set forth herein. Accordingly and in such event, the father shall immediately notify the mother of his inability to visit the children as originally contemplated and both parties shall use their best efforts to reach an accommodation so that the children's schedule is not unduly disrupted and so that the father's summer visitation is not unduly restricted. If, during the time that the father has the children with him pursuant to this summer visitation plan, he is called away on business and must, therefore, relinquish physical custody of the children, he shall be credited with those days upon his return from said business commitments, if any.

(f) The failure of the father to exercise the foregoing rights on one or more occasions shall in no event be deemed a waiver of such rights.

(g) The relinquishment of the custody of the children by the father to the mother as provided herein shall not be construed to operate as the father's consent to the adoption of the children by any other person, nor shall such relinquishment confer upon the mother any authority, in case of her death, to appoint a guardian for the child to the exclusion of the father.

Where to visit The place where the parent may visit with the children must also be carefully considered. Again it is important to be flexible. Usually the non-custodial parent picks up the children and takes them out to dinner or to the movies. These are fine diversions that are good for the children, but they do not often provide the optimum environment for parent–child discussions.

Comfortable environment If, for instance, a regular midweek visit can be arranged in their home, the children may be more comfortable and able to discuss their problems and concerns with the visiting parent. Restaurants and amusement parks may be fun, but there is a certain degree of artificiality that puts children on their guard. The home represents a better setting for the non-custodial spouse to appear as a parental figure, creating the possibility of more open discussions of such matters as problems in school, difficulties with a step-parent and adjusting to life after the divorce.

Demand reasonable visitation The non-custodial parent must demand a well-reasoned visitation schedule if it is not offered. Bitterness and anxiety should not control. Rather, one should negotiate visitation rights in the proper frame of mind, never losing sight that the children are the prime beneficiaries. It has often happened that a parent eager to be rid of a spouse and get the divorce over with pushes aside his or her responsibilities and love for a child by trading away visitation for a divorce. Years later, that hasty decision may prove almost impossible to reverse—legally and psychologically.

How does a court decide what kind of visitation to permit a parent to have with his or her children?

Various factors
The answer to this question is based more on practicalities and common sense than it is on legal considerations. Many factors go into making the decision, such as (1) your proximity to the custodial home; (2) your work schedule; (3) the ages of the children; (4) the custodial parent's schedule; (5) your financial means for travel, if you will be living far apart; and (6) the children's schedules and day-to-day commitments.

Counterbalancing rights
Judges try to allow the non-custodial parent to have as much time as possible with the child, but this must be counterbalanced with the custodial parent's rights. Visitation cannot be disruptive. Many judges will leave it to the parties to determine their own visitation schedule. After all, they are much closer to the situation and know their own needs and inclinations. Only when the parties cannot reach an accord will the judge reluctantly step in.

Retain flexibility
Any visitation arrangement, whether it be by agreement or court order, requires parental cooperation and flexibility in order for it to succeed. What was feasible at the time of the divorce may prove impractical five years later. Parents change, their commitments change and so do the needs of the children.

Will the judge allow me to take our four-year-old son from my wife's house on the days that I visit him, or will I be required to restrict the visitation to my wife's home?

Unrestricted visitation
Except in unusual circumstances, your visitation will not be so restricted. Generally, you are entitled to take the child away from the custodial residence. There may be some restrictions about leaving the state or extended overnight visits, and your wife's consent may be required in such situations. Otherwise, your time with your son will be unhampered so that your own relationship can develop.

Special circumstances
Visitation is limited to the custodial home only in circumstances where the child's age or health requires that the child remain there. In such cases, the custodial parent is required to stay away from home during the other parent's visit. Sometimes past misconduct and abuse by the non-custodial parent

in exercising visitation rights may require a court-ordered restriction.

Can a court grant visitation rights to the grandparents?

Yes. Regular visitation with grandparents is indeed in the child's best interests, so if a visitation order is necessary in this regard, a court will certainly grant one. Usually there is no problem with the custodial parent allowing both sets of grandparents to have reasonable access to the child. However, if the custodial parent refuses to allow such visitation, an application to court may be made for an order specifically permitting the grandparents adequate visitation.

Grandfather clause

I've heard of custody battles, but are there such things as visitation fights?

Unfortunately, yes. Some spouses never get over the idea of treating their children as pawns, and they use visitation as a psychological weapon, often with disastrous results.

John had always been late. Even the wedding ceremony had been delayed ten minutes. So after the divorce it should have come as no surprise to Marsha that the doorbell would ring sometimes an hour after John's weekend visitation was to have begun. For most, this should have been no more than a petty annoyance. Marsha, however, chose to make an issue of it, and she constantly berated John in front of the children over his tardiness. Apparently never having overcome the bitterness of their divorce, Marsha took pleasure in making John squirm under her verbal attacks. Worse yet, she would openly question John's love for his kids and threaten to deny him access to the home the next time he came late.

Discouraging visitation

The situation grew worse as time passed. Even on those rare occasions when John was on time, Marsha would find something else to complain about. One time, she ridiculed his taking the children the prior weekend to the ballet, claiming that he was trying to make the boys into homosexuals. Another time, John came home two hours late only to be met by two police officers who had been summoned by Marsha's hysterical accusations of "childnapping"; John and the children had been delayed in late-afternoon beach traffic.

John began to experience stomach pains. He visited his doctor, and he was told that he was definitely developing an ulcer and that his blood pressure was way above normal. It took

No legal recourse

only a moment for John and his doctor to conclude that his wife's harassment was responsible. The doctor, in fact, suggested that he skip a few weekends until his pressure came down. John consulted with his former attorney, but he was told that no court could put a gag on his wife. She was not really denying him visitation, only making it very difficult. There was no legal remedy.

As time passed, John missed more and more weekends with the children. He began to find other things to do with his free time. Marsha became concerned about his absences, and several times she telephoned him to ask that he try to visit the children the coming weekend. Invariably, he would come up with some excuse. Marsha had received reports from the counselor at school that her two boys were beginning to become disruptive, the cause of which was diagnosed as the absence of a male role model. Unfortunately, the die had already been cast. The worst part was that Marsha never fully understood what she had done.

How does a judge determine how much child support will be ordered?

Controlling factors

Beginning with the premise that child support is a *mutual* obligation, the court will consider such relevant factors as: (1) the financial resources of the custodial and non-custodial parent, as well as those of the children; (2) the physical and emotional health of the children, and their educational or vocational needs and aptitudes; (3) the standard of living the children would have enjoyed had the marriage not ended; (4) the tax consequences to the parties; and (5) the non-monetary contributions that the parents will make toward the care and well-being of the children.

The overriding concern is the best interests of the children and what the parents can reasonably be expected to afford. The court will not consider marital fault as a factor in making child support determinations.

Does a court have the power to order my husband to maintain medical insurance for the children in addition to the weekly support payments?

Medical insurance can be required

Yes. In most states a court can require a spouse to carry hospitalization and major medical insurance as part of the child support order. A court has many powers and wide discretion when it comes to fashioning child support. Certainly medical care is an important part of the support obligation, and by requiring insurance, the court helps assure that the children's needs will be met. If your husband had such insurance prior to the divorce, most judges will be quite inclined to require that he continue maintaining such coverage.

I really believe that our children should go to private school. Can the court order my husband to incur this expense?

A court may include in a child support order requirements *Elements of* providing necessary shelter, food, clothing, care, medical at- *child support* tention, education and other proper, reasonable expenses for the children. When it comes to private schooling, the courts are divided. Determinations are made on a case-by-case basis, but if circumstances can be shown that warrant the necessity of a private school education, most courts are empowered to direct a parent to incur such expenses.

In considering an application for the payment of private school expenses, a court will explore the parents' respective situations in life, the environment in which the children are *Court looks* reared and the father's financial ability. Other important con- *at needs and* siderations are whether the children have always attended pri- *family back-* vate schools, whether the father has previously approved of *ground* such education, the educational and social background of the parents and the children's academic ability. The court will also look to the availability of adequate substitute public education. If, upon reviewing these factors, a court determines that it is in the best interests of the children that they be afforded a private school education and that your husband has the ability to afford it, you may be entitled to such an order.

What about getting my husband to pay for our son's college tuition?

Once again, courts in most states can order a parent to pay for the child's college education if the circumstances warrant it. It will not happen automatically because a college education has traditionally been viewed as an extra and not a necessity. *Sometimes a* However, many courts have pointed to the increased value that *necessity* society places on a college education, and the old rule is eroding. Where the parent has the means to afford a college education, more judges are beginning to view it as a necessity. As with the issue of private schools, the court will consider the educational background of the parents, the child's academic ability and the father's financial means.

My children are eight and ten years old, and I want them to go to college. Can the court put in my divorce decree the requirement that my husband pay for it?

Must demonstrate need

It can, but it probably won't. Age is an important factor in determining the necessity of a college education. In all likelihood, your children have yet to demonstrate the needs and aptitudes for a college education. Your hopes, dreams and desires will not control. However, although the chances are remote, there is no harm in asking for such a provision in your divorce decree.

Renew application when children are older

As your children grow older, you can always renew your application to the court for the expenses of their college education. Divorce decrees are never final, and a court can always modify them as the situation warrants. In fact, most cases today concerning college expenses involve couples who come back to court many years after the divorce.

You say that divorce decrees are never final. Could you explain what you mean by that?

No crystal ball

Ordinarily, the only thing that is final in a divorce is the divorce itself. All the other provisions relating to maintenance, custody, visitation and child support can be modified in the future if there is a substantial change of circumstances. The law recognizes that no judge is omniscient. Instead, judges can only make a fair estimation based upon what is likely to occur. Circumstances may change. You or your spouse may find yourself in a different financial situation; one of the children may become seriously ill or require psychological therapy.

Sometimes the problem has nothing to do with dollars. The non-custodial parent may now feel that the children would be better off with him or her. The children may even articulate such a preference. The visitation schedule may need changing. Whatever the reason, either party is always free to petition the court for a modification of the divorce decree. He or she will have the burden of demonstrating that the changed circumstances were unanticipated and substantial. We save some other comments and observations on this topic of post-divorce problems for the final chapter.

Chapter Seven
NEGOTIATING A TRUCE

A divorce action does not have to go down to the wire. More times than not, it is the parties and their attorneys, and not the judge, who decide the final outcome of the collateral issues. Of course, in most states it is still up to the court to determine whether the parties are entitled to a divorce, and this depends upon the testimony that is offered on the witness stand. Nevertheless, judges are only too willing to forsake their Solomonic role and let the parties decide support, custody and other incidental relief.

The collateral issues can be negotiated and settled at any time. Once a divorce action is commenced, any pretrial agreement is called an *out-of-court settlement,* even though it may be reached in the judge's chambers or a corridor of the courthouse. Some couples are able to settle these matters well before a divorce action is started, by negotiating and executing a formal separation agreement.

OUT-OF-COURT SETTLEMENTS

Reasonable and fair spouses usually reach a negotiated settlement of the collateral issues at some point in the divorce proceedings. There are many advantages to such settlements, both legally and emotionally. Some clients are very apprehensive that their lawyer is "selling them down the river" by suggesting a settlement. Often they lose sight of the fact that the goal is a fair resolution of all issues, and instead look at a divorce proceeding as some modern form of public stock in which to punish and embarrass their spouse.

The parties themselves are in the best position to determine their respective financial needs and means. Their approach will be much more tailored than the court's, and often more creative. Indeed, in title states, where the court's power with respect to property divisions is severely circumscribed, a party can obtain more diverse and sometimes greater relief by settling out of court than would otherwise be possible.

Does an out-of-court settlement have as much validity as a judge's decision?

Final resolution

Yes. A settlement is a resolution of all the issues in the divorce action by the voluntary agreement of the parties. The terms of the settlement become part of the divorce decree.

Rid yourself of winner-take-all philosophy

Some people mistakenly draw a negative inference from the term "settling a case." They feel that winning is all that matters, and for them settlement is a capitulation to the other's demands. This is unrealistic. Rarely is a divorce case so black and white, and although a settlement involves compromise on both sides, it does not mean surrender or that you are settling for something that is against your best interests. Certain provisions in the settlement may favor the other spouse, but these will usually be balanced against terms to your advantage.

Agreement accepted by judge

A settlement agreement involves all the issues in the divorce action. This includes the divorce itself—who is going to get it and on what grounds it will be based—as well as the other elements discussed in the previous chapters. If the terms of the parties' settlement are fair and reasonable, the judge will accept and approve the settlement, which is then as fully binding and valid as if the judge had reached his or her own decision after a complete trial.

What do you mean that the terms of the settlement must be fair and reasonable? Can't my wife and I agree to anything we want?

Some judicial scrutiny possible

Although you and your wife will have great latitude in reaching a settlement, there are restrictions. This is especially true when children are involved.

Anxious moments

Mary's divorce trial was scheduled for the next week. She sat nervously in her office awaiting her attorney's telephone call. He was calling to tell her the time and the room number for the trial, but she was really hoping that he would have word that her husband had accepted the latest settlement offer. She knew that the trial would be messy. Her husband's attorney had sub-poenaed her present lover, and the adultery case against her seemed a foregone conclusion.

Mary remembered the prior evening's conversation with David, her boyfriend. He was upset. He did not look forward to taking the witness stand, and he repeatedly asked if there was any way that he could get out of it and whether she and her husband could settle the case without going to trial. Mary replied that her lawyer was doing his best, but so far the prospects for settling looked dismal. Her husband still refused to pay adequate child support.

Mary looked at her watch. It was already four o'clock, and she had not yet heard from her lawyer. She began thinking about the promotion that she was expecting by the end of the year. Her impending divorce appeared to have had no ill effects on her prospects, but she knew that if word ever leaked out about her affair, her rapid rise in the company could be set back. Suddenly she swung her chair around, resolutely picked up the telephone and dialed her lawyer. She was surprised to get through to him immediately.

"Hello, Mary, I was just about to call you. Your husband has upped child support another $10 a week, but I think he still has a long way to go."

"I don't care," Mary replied. "Take it. Call his lawyer and let's wrap up the whole thing."

"Are you kidding? The child support is woefully inadequate. He should be paying at least twice that."

"Maybe he should, but I don't think it's worth going through with the whole thing just to prove the point. Besides, I know I'll be getting the promotion, and I'll have plenty of money to provide for my own kids."

Her lawyer stayed on the phone another fifteen minutes trying to persuade her not to accept the offer. However, she remained adamant, and his efforts were unavailing. Reluctantly, he later called his adversary and told him that it appeared that the parties had reached a settlement.

The parties and their attorneys arrived in court the following week as scheduled. When the case was called, the husband's attorney informed the judge that the case had been settled. Commending them for their efforts, the judge asked to hear the terms of the settlement. He interrupted the husband's attorney when he got to the child support provision, asking him how much the parties each earned. The judge paused for a moment, and then called both attorneys to the bench. He pointed out that the husband's child support obligation represented less than ten percent of his gross income—an income that was twice the wife's. He told the lawyers that he could not accept the settlement; it was not in the best interests of the children.

Mary's attorney explained that his client expected a promotion and a considerable raise. The judge replied that he was not interested in possibilities. He did not want to see her in court a few months later bringing a motion for increased child support if her promotion did not come through. Besides, he believed that the husband should be paying more money anyway, and he said that the husband's allegations of adultery, even if proved, should have no bearing on the issue of child support. He told the lawyers to go outside and try to come up with an arrangement that more closely reflected the parties' respective incomes.

As Mary listened to her lawyer, she began to realize that she was sacrificing her children's welfare for her own expediency. Her resolve to go to trial if her husband did not come up with an acceptable offer grew stronger. Meanwhile, her husband was learning from his attorney that the judge had not been impressed with the adultery allegation and that their "trump card" had become a joker. The issue of child support would be decided on finances alone, and his wife's wrongdoing would not be considered, especially by this judge.

Later that afternoon, the judge happily accepted the revised settlement that the parties had reached.

At the beginning of the case my lawyer was demanding $150 a week for maintenance. He has just telephoned me and said that my husband is willing to settle for $120. He says that this is a good deal, that he asked for more than we could probably get anyway. I'm not so sure, and I would like to know if you have any guidelines on when to accept a settlement offer?

Financial information crucial

You should settle a case only after you have received adequate financial disclosure from your spouse and believe that the terms of the settlement are fair and reasonable.

The art of negotiation

Too many clients confuse their lawyer's early demands with what they are ultimately entitled to. As attorneys, we often demand more than we expect, because this gives everyone some negotiating room and flexibility. Also, at the beginning of the case, when there has yet to be a chance for financial discovery, an attorney does not know the true picture, so it is always better to err on the high side in taking a position. In negotiations, it is easy to go down, virtually impossible to go up.

Too much better than too little

Acceptance should not be a visceral reaction. Fear of trial, anxiety, anger and depression have no place in the determination. The settlement should be based on a reasonable estimation of your present and anticipated needs.

Is it true that eighty-five percent of contested divorces are ultimately settled before going to trial?

Actually, the percentage is higher than that. The advantages of settlement soon become apparent to litigating spouses. There may even be a mathematical formula that shows that emotions begin to cool and heads become more reasonable as the parties walk up each of the courthouse steps. As the case comes closer to trial, the chances for settlement are enhanced. Finally, as we have already explained, most judges make concerted efforts to arrange a settlement in a pretrial conference.

Most cases settled

I really think that my lawyer is selling me down the river; the settlement offer stinks! What do I do now?

Don't accept the offer.

We assume that you are not overreacting and that the terms of the offer appear unreasonable. We suggest that you meet with your attorney and discuss the proposed settlement and your reasons for rejecting it. Remember, just because your lawyer has informed you of a settlement offer does not mean that he or she endorses it or has accepted it on your behalf. Attorneys have an obligation to pass on to clients all settlement and compromise offers. Recommendations, advice and opinions come later. This is why you have a lawyer. If your attorney does not recommend a settlement, this signals uneasiness and indicates the need for more detailed discussion between the two of you.

Lawyer obligated to pass along all offers

Work with your lawyer

If your attorney does recommend a particular settlement, but you are still uncomfortable with it, you are free to seek a second professional opinion. Do not ask your butcher. Ultimately the decision is yours, and no lawyer can make it for you. If you get a sense that your lawyer is indeed throwing in the towel, which happens a lot more rarely than people think, then perhaps it is time to find someone in whom you have more faith and confidence.

Only you can make final decision

What if I change my mind later? Can an out-of-court settlement be modified or renegotiated?

Modification by mutual consent

A settlement, like a divorce decree, is not final. It can always be modified or renegotiated by the consent of *both* parties.

A *unilateral* modification is another story. It requires a formal motion or application to the court with notice to your former spouse. Sometimes a post-trial hearing is required. Most post-divorce modification applications concern either monetary support or child custody. The party seeking the modification must demonstrate sufficiently changing circumstances from the time the settlement was entered into. In some instances, the party must even go further and show that the changed circumstances were either unanticipated or extraordinary.

May need to make motion to modify

Proof of unanticipated and changed circumstances

Is it a fact that a settlement may be reached even after the trial has started?

Case can be settled anytime

Yes. A divorce case may be settled at any time, and it is not uncommon for the attorneys and their clients to reach an accord after the trial has started. This actual case history is illustrative:

For example:

It had been seven tortuous months, but the case was finally ready for trial. All through the various stages of the case there had been offers and counteroffers communicated by both sides, but none had been accepted.

The trial began and Robert's wife took the stand. For most of the morning she described in graphic detail the alleged brutality of her husband.

Robert turned to his lawyer and urgently whispered, "I can't believe what she's saying!" His lawyer merely nodded his head and continued to scribble notes on his yellow pad.

After the lunch break Elizabeth's testimony continued, each sentence apparently more damaging than the next. Finally, her lawyer turned to Robert's and said with a sneer, "Your witness, counselor."

Mr. Singer approached the witness and asked Elizabeth in a barely audible voice, "But, ma'am, throughout your testimony I didn't hear one word about your paramour, Joseph Foster. Where is he?"

As Elizabeth's attorney rose to his feet to object, the door to the courtroom opened and a man slowly entered. It was the long-missing Mr. Foster. By a lucky coincidence Robert's lawyer had discovered the whereabouts of the elusive lover and had served a witness subpoena on him that very morning, compelling his appearance in court. The amazing timing of Mr. Foster's appearance was also lucky. The bailiff hurriedly escorted the potential witness from the courtroom, but the damage had already been done.

Elizabeth's attorney hastily convened a conference for purposes of settling. Obviously, the testimony of Mr. Foster would have been too damaging to his client's case.

The settlement was reached approximately forty-five minutes later, and Robert had just lived a poignant example of the legal maxim: "Until the judge judges, it is never too late to settle."

SEPARATION AGREEMENTS

Many couples prefer ending their marriage in increments. The first step is a legal separation, which is accomplished in most states by signing a formal *separation agreement.* Invariably the separation agreement resolves most of the collateral issues involving support and children, and it specifies that these provisions will continue after the divorce.

What is a separation agreement?

A separation agreement is a written contract that is entered into before spouses are divorced. The agreement specifically sets forth the rights and obligations of each party. The two vital elements are contained in the words "separation" and "agreement"; the parties must have actually stopped living together and they must have reached an understanding about how their relationship will be redefined. *A written contract*

A separation agreement modifies the so-called "marriage contract." Unbeknownst to few, marriage brings with it certain legal rights and obligations. Many of these are statutorily defined. For example, there are conjugal rights, giving each spouse the right to be with the other. There are automatic estate rights and, of course, the whole panoply of support, maintenance and property rights that we have been discussing throughout this book. A separation agreement terminates or modifies them. Moreover, the agreement contains the future obligations of the parties. *Redefines marriage contract*

My wife and I have been separated for over two years. I met a lawyer at the club, and he told me that we should have a written agreement. What is your advice?

We favor and encourage written separation agreements. The parties' respective expectations are frozen, and their informal understandings are much less likely to be misunderstood. Even where there are no assets, property or children, the agreement evidences the separation, which may provide an independent ground for getting the divorce. A separation agreement also gives the parties the opportunity to reach a settlement before a divorce action has even started. The terms of the separation agreement are comprehensive, and they may control everything from custody to who gets the silverware. All that is left for the court to do is grant the divorce.

Less likelihood of misunderstanding

Provides vehicle for pretrial settlement

Just what are the advantages of a separation agreement?

A separation agreement has at least three distinct advantages. First, the couple maintains *control* over their own financial and property rights. The agreement controls, and a judge will not have to determine the legal rights of the parties. Closely tied to control is *privacy,* which is the second advantage of a separation agreement. Couples who are forced into court must subject their finances and intimate details of the marriage to a judge's close scrutiny. There is less agony in negotiating a separation agreement than there is in sitting through a trial. The parties can more easily focus on their future needs and not the recriminations that are part of a broken marriage.

Control factor

Privacy factor

The third, and perhaps most significant, advantage is the positive effect that a separation agreement can have on the post-divorce relationship. Couples who *plan* this relationship by discussing openly such issues as finances, property rights, custody and visitation often create a bond that is stronger and more meaningful than anything that a judge can fashion. Family counselors and psychiatrists are virtually unanimous in their view that open discussion of such topics leads to a sturdier framework on which to base a longer-lasting post-divorce relationship. If there are children involved, this is a very important consideration.

Relationship planning

Establishing solid post-divorce relationship

Do I need a lawyer to draft a separation agreement or can my wife and I do it ourselves?

While you may be able to do it yourselves, we strongly advise against it.

Certainly you and your wife should initially discuss the broad elements of your separation agreement before retaining an attorney. Just as we encourage open discussions at the beginning of a divorce action, the same holds true for those contemplating a separation agreement. However, a time comes when your understandings should be formalized in a written agreement, and that is the time for an attorney. *Discuss details . . . . . . Get lawyer to incorporate*

Do the terms of a separation agreement continue to be valid after a divorce is obtained?

Yes. That is the whole idea. All separation agreements contain languge specifiying that the terms are to be incorporated and made a part of the divorce decree. *Agreement survives*

What areas should be covered in a separation agreement?

Of course, the answer depends on your particular situation. However, all of the significant issues and concerns of your marriage should be encompassed in the agreement. If you have children, the separation agreement must contain a provision for their custody, visitation and support. The latter can also include college education, should the parties so agree, as well as health insurance and summer camps. The division of marital property will also be specifically provided for, as will maintenance, should there be a need for it. A separation agreement can also provide for the temporary occupancy of the marital home until the children are emancipated, or some other event. Like any contract, the separation agreement may also include certain provisions that go beyond marital rights, such as an agreement to make a last will in favor of the other or to maintain a child as a beneficiary on an insurance policy. *Agreement is tailored to your particular needs*

Because most separation agreements are drafted as comprehensive and complete documents, it is important that you and your attorney be sure to include provisions that reasonably anticipate and provide for future events. We suggest that you consult with this checklist to make sure that all the bases are covered:

☐ property division
☐ (temporary) occupancy and upkeep of marital home
☐ responsibility for joint debts and future liability
☐ lump sum payments in lieu of certain property divisions
☐ interest in family business, or payments in alternative

- [ ] maintenance—amount and duration, or lump sum settlement
- [ ] child custody and visitation
- [ ] child support, education and emancipation events
- [ ] health care
- [ ] insurance (health and life)
- [ ] taxes and deductions
- [ ] estate rights—discharge and agreement to make a will
- [ ] full financial disclosure
- [ ] mutual releases and discharge of non-divorce claims
- [ ] modification
- [ ] resolution of future disputes concerning agreement by arbitration (optional)

Can the terms of a separation agreement be changed later on?

Changing terms by further agreement

Yes, by *mutual* agreement. Most separation agreements provide that the terms can be freely amended, but that all such modifications must be in writing and signed by both parties. However, when only one person wants a change, the procedure gets more complicated since courts are extremely reluctant to interfere with private contracts.

Modification for children's sake

This is a good time to point out an exception to that last statement. The terms in the agreement that affect children may be modified by a court on the application of either party. The children are not deemed parties to the contract (they never signed it), so that if unanticipated and extraordinary circumstances arise in the future, a court has the power to make different provisions than those originally contained in the separation agreement.

PHASE III:
THE CONTINUUM

Chapter Eight
POST-DIVORCE PROBLEMS

It often comes as a terrible shock, but many former spouses soon discover that the divorce decree is not necessarily the end of the relationship, just the end of the marriage. In fact, a divorce is but one element of a continuum. Long after the divorce, legal rights and liabilities can be redefined, tested and perhaps extinguished as both external and internal circumstances tip the scale in one direction or the other.

In all but the simplest cases, the divorce decree or settlement is not the final step. Whenever children, support and prospective property divisions are included, a divorce marks the beginning of an entirely new, often unanticipated and sometimes difficult relationship between the former spouses. This should never be forgotten. Too many times we have seen one party press his or her legal and psychological advantage far beyond what was required, destroying in the process whatever possibility existed for a post-divorce relationship based on respect and concern.

No one "wins" in a divorce. The very fact that a union conceived in love and hope metamorphoses into the traumatic experience that is antiseptically called "dissolution" should give pause to anyone who believes that they will walk away from the divorce completely unscathed. There are no victors in the matrimonial arena, and the spouse who views the psychological or financial ruin of the other as cause for celebration is indeed a seriously misguided individual. Without sounding unduly mystical, it has been our experience that what you "send out" during a divorce has a way of coming back to you later.

Your approach to the divorce process and its final resolution is crucial. Expect to come away with a fair and reasonable return on your investment—the marriage. Be pragmatic, not emotional. We fully understand how difficult this can be, and it is a very rare client who totally succeeds. But this is where your efforts should be directed, not in seeking retribution. No court can grant emotional relief, and it is foolish to expect the divorce decree to mete out spousal punishment in the form of public flogging or the like. Instead it makes better sense to work toward maintaining an amicable, workable relationship with your former spouse.

CHILDREN

Children require a good post-divorce relationship that encourages the non-custodial parent to fulfill his or her parental and financial obligations. We have already seen that children who have regular contact and ready access to the other parent find divorce less traumatic. Visitation should therefore be permitted as much as possible, even if it means occasionally stretching the letter of the visitation provisions. Both parents should be cooperative and flexible, striving to create an optimum environment for the children's healthy relationship with them. This applies as well to the financial side of the coin— child support.

No attorney or judge can foresee every possibility in formulating a divorce settlement or decree. Conditions and needs change. An adequate child support provision may erode in time and become barely tolerable as the ravages of inflation and the increasing needs of the children take their toll. A special unanticipated expense may arise that was not covered in the separation agreement, for which the custodial parent now needs financial assistance from the former spouse. Maryanne found herself in just that situation. She and her husband had executed a detailed separation agreement before the divorce, which was finalized six years ago. Donald, her former husband, agreed to pay $150 weekly child support for the two children, as well as maintaining health insurance and contributing up to $750 annually for clothing.

Donald continued to maintain a good relationship with their two daughters. Although she had exclusive custody and control, Maryanne always made sure to consult with him about any decisions regarding the children's care and education. Thus it was not unexpected when Maryanne telephoned her former husband to tell him that she was going to have Sally, their youngest, tested by a speech therapist. Both had noticed lately that Sally's verbal skills were not progressing and that recently she had developed a lisp. Donald agreed.

Two weeks later, Dr. Jacobson met with both parents and suggested that Sally begin immediate therapy. The disorder was correctable, in his opinion, as long as treatment was started immediately. The projected cost of the therapy was about $2,000. Maryanne explained that she would first like to discuss it with her former husband and that she would telephone the doctor the following day. She and Donald decided to talk about it over a cup of coffee at the Howard Johnson's off the interstate.

Ordinarily, she would have proposed that they split the expense evenly, since as a freelance photographer she earned about as much as Donald, who had higher expenses since remarrying. However, she had recently invested a bundle in new equipment, and she was strapped. She asked Donald whether he could afford Sally's therapy alone. He said that he really could not, but that he was sure something could be worked out. After mulling it over, he proposed that he contribute the $1,500 that he had managed to save the past several years and, if necessary, borrow the rest on his Ready Credit checking account. He would repay the loan monthly by deducting a portion from the child support payments. Meanwhile, whenever Maryanne got a large fee for an assignment, she could pay him back part of the other $500. Maryanne accepted, even though it would probably mean serving a few more macaroni and cheese dinners every month.

Science fiction? No. There are indeed couples who can work out such post-divorce problems without resorting to lawyers and the courts. Had Donald refused to contribute anything toward Sally's therapy, Maryanne might have been forced to commence a post-divorce proceeding for a modification of the original child support provisions. In all likelihood, Dr. Jacobson would have had to testify about the speech defect, the necessity of the proposed therapy and the prospects for success; his expert-witness fee might have been in excess of $500 just for that appearance. Maryanne would also have had to incur legal fees. Given the rough equality of their income, it is unlikely that the court would have required Donald to pay for her lawyer.

In some states, the requirements for modifying separation agreements are quite strict, and Maryanne would have had to establish that the financial circumstances had changed extraordinarily and were entirely unanticipated at the time the agreement was signed. Assuming that she could sustain her burden of proof, which is probable in this case, the judge's decision in her favor may not have been rendered for several months. All she would have had at that point was a court order, which she could not use to pay Dr. Jacobson. If Donald refused to obey the court order, Maryanne would have had to start enforcement and contempt proceedings, consuming more time. Meanwhile, unless Dr. Jacobson agreed to proceed without payment, Sally's needed therapy would have been postponed.

A working post-divorce relationship certainly benefited Maryanne and Donald. They avoided the expense and acrimony of further litigation, but the real beneficiary was their daughter Sally, who began her therapy the following week and is doing quite well. If parents can forget the past and focus on the children's present needs, the result is more often than not a practical and immediate solution to the particular issue at hand. Even the little "emergencies," like not being able to find a babysitter and needing the other parent to fill in at the last minute, are readily resolved. The alternative is disruptive, harmful acrimony, often involving post-divorce litigation.

If former spouses cannot work out new difficulties and unanticipated changes, they soon find themselves once again climbing those courthouse steps, this time to commence an enforcement or modification proceeding. We cannot possibly give detailed information about these proceedings within the confines of this book; however, we can summarize them in the remainder of the chapter, highlighting their pitfalls and difficulties, all with an idea of conveying to you an important maxim: Try to get everything right the first time and maintain a rational relationship with your former spouse, so that if unforeseen problems arise, you can work them out yourselves.

ENFORCEMENT PROCEEDINGS

Failure to look beyond the divorce, blithely ignoring the continuum, means for many going back to court time and time again. The most common post-divorce problem is the suspension or termination of maintenance and child support payments. Unless lines of communication remain open, the financially dependent party has no alternative other than to initiate an enforcement proceeding. He or she makes an application or motion to the court for an order compelling the other party to pay the arrearages, i.e., the money owed. Depending on the parties' respective financial circumstances, the court order may also require the remiss former spouse to pay for all or part of the other's counsel fees.

The providing party, in other words, the one who has the obligation to pay maintenance or support, frequently cross-claims in these proceedings for a modification of the divorce decree or settlement to reduce the original financial obligation. The claim is based upon an imagined or real downturn in his or her income. This usually entails updated financial disclosures, such as filing affidavits of net worth by both sides, and in many instances an evidentiary hearing on the parties' finances. The procedure can become quite burdensome, and a final determination may not be forthcoming for several months.

MODIFICATION PROCEEDINGS

What was eight years ago an adequate amount of weekly support may have been reduced to a mere pittance by our infamous double-digit inflation of the past several years. Ten years ago, the wife was unemployed; now she is a regional vice-president of a large paper manufacturing concern earning $55,000 a year. In both cases, a post-divorce court application for modification—upward or downward—of the original child support and maintenance provisions may be necessary if the parties are unable to discuss the changed circumstances candidly and cooperate toward achieving a fair and mutual agreement. The proceeding again requires financial disclosure and, most likely, a hearing. The party seeking the modification must show at the very least substantially changed circumstances. Oddly enough, many courts have held that inflation alone is an insufficient reason for a modification. The rationale used is that inflation adversely affects both parties; as the consumer price index climbs, so do the expenses of the providing party.

The petitioning party must introduce evidence of changed financial needs, employment, income and other such factors that have independently enhanced or diminished the parties' finances. If this burden is met, the court will order an appropriate modification of the original decree. This is permitted because divorce decrees, unlike other judgments, are never final, and the collateral provisions concerning support, maintenance, custody, visitation and the like can be changed anytime if the circumstances warrant it. Remember that separation agreements are different and are much more difficult to modify without both parties' written consent.

CUSTODY AND VISITATION

Modifying established custody rights in a divorce decree is also difficult. Generally, a court will not disturb an existing continuous custody arrangement unless the petitioner can demonstrate that the custodial parent has become unfit. Proving this is much harder than it sounds, and many factors are taken into consideration. Judges are loath to change custody, and they must be convinced that it would be in "the best interests" of the children—the universal rule. The traditional rule is that prior custody decrees and agreements are given tremendous weight and, unless there are *extraordinary* circumstances, are rarely overturned. Courts will not view the parties' rights as presumptively equal, as if writing on a clean slate, and the custodial parent has a distinct advantage. However, this philosophy is gradually eroding, and the trend in several states is to focus on the best interests of the children without requiring proof of an extraordinary change of circumstances.

Frequently, after the passage of time, children express a desire to live with the other parent, which is not too surprising when you consider that the task of disciplining and supervising them usually falls squarely on the shoulders of the custodial parent. Courts have long recognized the importance of the children's stated preferences, especially as they grow older, but they have regularly noted that "the desires of young children, capable of distortive manipulation by a bitter or perhaps even well-meaning parent, do not always reflect the long-term best interests of the children" (*Matter of Nehra* v. *Uhlar* 43 N.Y. 2d 242, 249). Circumstances that courts have relied upon to award a change of custody include alcoholism, drug addiction, unmarried cohabitation (living with someone of the opposite sex), homosexuality and child abuse. Sometimes the reasoning may be less obvious. In one recent decision, the judge ordered a change of custody to the father because the mother, in derogation of her original promise, had been lax in providing the children with a strict religious upbringing.

Enforcing prior custody rights is a somewhat less common but nonetheless important area. It occurs when the non-custodial parent either abuses his or her visitation rights or completely disregards the custodial rights of the other parent—in other words, "childnapping." In most states there are criminal sanctions that can be brought against the spouse who wrongfully takes or retains actual custody of the children.

Sometimes disputes arise between parents who rigidly adhere to specified visitation schedules and refuse to adjust as situations change. One parent may not feel that he or she is being permitted enough time with the children, while the custodial parent may discover that overly frequent visitation is disruptive of the family environment. Consequently, if the parents are unable to resolve these difficulties between themselves, either may commence a proceeding to modify the visitation rights. Once again, the courts will attempt to determine the issue by focusing upon those considerations that promote the children's welfare; the needs of the parents are secondary.

Many non-custodial parents are wrongfully denied access to their children. They often do not realize that they can go to court to enforce the visitation rights that they were previously granted. Courts are receptive to such applications because they believe that it is in the children's best interests that frequent contact be maintained with both parents. A parent may find himself or herself denied visitation by the custodial parent. Such conduct is generally viewed as reprehensible in the absence of extraordinary circumstances such as physical abuse. The "locked out" parent may commence a visitation enforcement proceeding, in which a court will order that prescribed visitation occur. Most judges put "teeth" in the order by including *linkage:* excusing child support obligations until visitation is resumed.

A common post-divorce visitation problem arises when the custodial spouse announces plans to move out of state. The other parent then attempts to obtain a court injunction prohibiting him or her from moving away with the children. An argument is presented to the judge that the move would effectively terminate or severely constrain the petitioning parent's visitation rights, since the time and cost of travel would be prohibitive. We have encountered a few cases where such an injunction was granted, largely because the custodial parent's motive for moving was neither a bona fide career change nor a new spouse's requirements, but rather whim and unsubstantiated hopes "for a better life" in a new locale. If the reasons for moving are sound, the injunction will likely be denied, but we are seeing more and more decisions in which the custodial parent is compelled to pay for the other's round-trip airfare one or more times a year.

CONCLUDING REMARKS

If you stop to think that more than half of the couples who get divorced end up back in court on any one of the numerous post-divorce issues just discussed, you should begin to appreciate the truth of our initial statement that divorce only ends the marriage, not the relationship. Couples who understand this concept spare themselves needless trauma, time and expense when unanticipated problems crop up. These are the couples who can still talk reasonably with one another and who strive to solve their problems in a caring and equitable fashion. These are indeed the lucky couples, but then again, after reading this book, you certainly have gained the wherewithal to join their ranks. The choice is yours.

APPENDIX:
STATE DIVORCE LAWS

**Grounds for Divorce
and Distribution of Marital Property**

Please note: This appendix should be used as a guide only. Divorce statutes are constantly in flux, and changes may have occurred in your state's laws which require explanation by an attorney licensed in your jurisdiction.

ALABAMA
Grounds: (a) Adultery
            (b) Drug addiction
            (c) Felony imprisonment for two years of a seven-year sentence
            (d) Infamous crime
            (e) Insanity
            (f) Irretrievable breakdown
            (g) Lack of capacity to consent to marriage
            (h) Separation of two years (one year in favor of wife only)
            (i) Unnatural or abnormal sex act with person of same or opposite sex or with a beast

Property Distribution: Equitable Distribution

ALASKA
Grounds: (a) Adultery
            (b) Cruel and inhuman treatment

(c) Drug addiction
(d) Habitual gross drunkenness since marriage and continuing one year prior to commencement of action
(e) Incompatibility of temperament
(f) Incurable mental illness where spouse has been confined to an institution for at least eighteen months
(g) Felony conviction
(h) Personal indignities
(i) Willful desertion for a period of one year

Property Distribution: Equitable Distribution

ARIZONA

Grounds: (a) Irretrievable breakdown

Property Distribution: Community Property (marital fault immaterial)

ARKANSAS

Grounds: (a) Impotency (at time of marriage and continuing)
(b) Willful desertion for one year without reasonable cause
(c) Felony conviction or other infamous crime
(d) Habitual drunkenness for one year
(e) Cruel and barbarous treatment that endangers the other spouse's life or results in indignities to the other spouse that renders the condition intolerable
(f) Adultery
(g) Bigamy
(h) Living separate and apart for three consecutive years voluntarily or by mutual consent
(i) Living separate and apart for three years because of spouse's incurable insanity
(j) Willful failure to support spouse while having the ability to provide necessaries of life

Property Distribution: Equitable Distribution

CALIFORNIA
Grounds: (a) Incurable insanity
              (b) Irretrievable breakdown
Property Distribution: Community Property

COLORADO
Grounds: (a) Irretrievable breakdown
Property Distribution: Equitable Distribution

CONNECTICUT
Grounds: (a) Separation or absence of eighteen months
              (b) Life imprisonment or infamous crime that violated conjugal duty that is punishable by imprisonment of more than one year
              (c) Irretrievable breakdown
              (d) Living separate and apart by reason of incompatibility for at least eighteen months immediately preceding the commencement of the action
              (e) Adultery
              (f) Willful desertion for one year with total neglect of marital duties
              (g) Habitual intemperance
              (h) Legal confinement in a hospital or institution because of mental illness for at least an aggregate period of five years within the six years immediately preceding the date of the complaint
Property Distribution: Equitable Distribution

DELAWARE
Grounds: (a) Irretrievable breakdown
Property Distribution: Equitable Distribution

FLORIDA
Grounds: (a) Irretrievable breakdown
              (b) Mental incompetence
Property Distribution: Equitable Distribution

GEORGIA
Grounds: (a) Felony conviction involving moral turpitude and two-year sentence

(b) Incurable mental illness for two years
(c) Irretrievable breakdown
(d) Intermarriage by persons within the prohibited degrees of consanguinity or affinity
(e) Impotency at the time of marriage
(f) Wife's pregnancy by another person at time of marriage that is unknown to husband
(g) Adultery
(h) Willful and continued desertion by either for at least one year
(i) Habitual intoxication
(j) Cruel and inhuman treatment

Property Distribution: Equitable Distribution

HAWAII

Grounds: (a) Separation of two years after separation decree or execution of a properly filed and executed separation agreement
(b) Irretrievable breakdown

Property Distribution: Equitable Distribution

IDAHO

Grounds: (a) Separation or absence of five years
(b) Felony conviction or imprisonment
(c) Incompatibility
(d) Irretrievable breakdown
(e) Adultery
(f) Extreme cruelty
(g) Habitual intemperance
(h) Permanent insanity
(i) Willful neglect

Property Distribution: Community Property

ILLINOIS

Grounds: (a) Bigamy
(b) Felony conviction or imprisonment
(c) Drug addiction for two years
(d) Infamous crime
(e) Impotency
(f) Adultery
(g) Willful desertion or absence for one year
(h) Habitual drunkenness for two years

(i) Extreme and repeated physical or mental cruelty

Property Distribution: Equitable Distribution

INDIANA
Grounds: (a) Infamous crime
(b) Irretrievable breakdown
(c) Impotency
(d) Incurable insanity for at least two years

Property Distribution: Equitable Distribution

IOWA
Grounds: (a) Irretrievable breakdown

Property Distribution: Equitable Distribution

KANSAS
Grounds: (a) Adultery
(b) Cruelty
(c) Habitual drunkenness
(d) Felony conviction or imprisonment
(e) Incompatibility

Property Distribution: Equitable Distribution

KENTUCKY
Grounds: (a) Irretrievable breakdown

Property Distribution: Equitable Distribution

LOUISIANA
Grounds: (a) Adultery
(b) Continuous separation for one year
(c) Conviction of a felony and death sentence or imprisonment with hard labor

Property Distribution: Equitable Distribution

MAINE
Grounds: (a) Irreconcilable differences
(b) Adultery
(c) Impotency
(d) Extreme cruelty
(e) Complete desertion for three consecutive years
(f) Gross and confirmed habits of intoxication from liquor or drugs
(g) Non-support or wanton neglect
(h) Cruel and abusive treatment

(i) Mental illness for at least seven consecutive years

Property Distribution: Equitable Distribution

MARYLAND
Grounds: (a) Separation, either voluntarily (one year) or involuntarily (three years)
(b) Felony conviction or imprisonment
(c) Living apart for one year pursuant to a judgment of separation
(d) Impotency
(e) Adultery
(f) Abandonment for at least one year

Property Distribution: Equitable Distribution (court cannot distribute property but may make a monetary award in lieu thereof)

MASSACHUSETTS
Grounds: (a) Adultery
(b) Impotency
(c) Complete desertion for one year
(d) Gross and confirmed habits of intoxication caused by voluntary excessive use of liquor or drugs
(e) Cruel and abusive treatment
(f) Irretrievable breakdown
(g) Gross, wanton and cruel refusal or neglect to provide suitable support, despite sufficient financial ability to do so

Property Distribution: Equitable Distribution

MICHIGAN
Grounds: (a) Irretrievable breakdown
Property Distribution: Equitable Distribution

MINNESOTA
Grounds: (a) Irretrievable breakdown
Property Distribution: Equitable Distribution

MISSISSIPPI
Grounds: (a) Bigamy
(b) Felony conviction or imprisonment

(c) Drug addiction

(d) Cruel and inhuman treatment

(e) Intermarriage by persons within prohibited degrees of consanguinity or affinity

(f) Irreconcilable differences

(g) Natural impotency

(h) Adultery

(i) Desertion for one year

(j) Habitual drunkenness

(k) Insanity at time of marriage if other party was unaware

(l) Incurable insanity

Property Distribution: Title State

MISSOURI

Grounds: (a) Separation for two years or one year if without consent

(b) Irretrievable breakdown

Property Distribution: Equitable Distribution

MONTANA

Grounds: (a) Irretrievable breakdown

Property Distribution: Equitable Distribution

NEBRASKA

Grounds: (a) Irretrievable breakdown

Property Distribution: Equitable Distribution

NEVADA

Grounds: (a) One-year separation or absence

(b) Incompatibility

(c) Insanity existing for two years

Property Distribution: Community Property

NEW HAMPSHIRE

Grounds: (a) Two years' separation or absence

(b) Felony conviction and actual imprisonment of at least one year

(c) Two years' absence without any contact

(d) Joining a religious sect or society that professes that marital relationship is unlawful, combined with a refusal to cohabit for at least six months

      (e) Wife resides out of state for ten years without husband's consent and fails to return to claim marital rights

      (f) Wife is an alien or citizen of another state who, after residing in New Hampshire for two years, leaves country with intention of becoming a citizen of a foreign country and fails to return to claim marital rights

      (g) Living apart voluntarily (one year) or involuntarily (three years)

      (h) Irreconcilable differences

      (i) Impotency

      (j) Adultery

      (k) Extreme cruelty or treating the other so as to seriously injure health or render cohabitation unreasonable

Property Distribution: Equitable Distribution

NEW JERSEY

Grounds: (a) Eighteen months' separation or absence

      (b) Felony conviction or imprisonment for eighteen months

      (c) Drug addiction for at least one year

      (d) Deviant sexual conduct

      (e) Adultery

      (f) Desertion

      (g) Extreme cruelty

      (h) Institutionalization for mental illness

      (i) Irretrievable breakdown

Property Distribution: Equitable Distribution

NEW MEXICO

Grounds: (a) Incompatibility

      (b) Irretrievable breakdown

Property Distribution: Community Property

NEW YORK

Grounds: (a) Abandonment for at least one year

      (b) Living apart pursuant to a written separation agreement or separation judgment for at least one year

      (c) Imprisonment for at least three years

(d) Cruel and inhuman treatment

(e) Adultery

Property Distribution: Equitable Distribution

NORTH CAROLINA

Grounds:

(a) One-year separation or absence

(b) Felony conviction or imprisonment for one year

(c) Deviant sexual conduct

(d) Living apart for three consecutive years by reason of incurable insanity

(e) Adultery

(f) Impotency

(g) Wife's pregnancy by another person at time of marriage of which husband is unaware

Property Distribution: Equitable Distribution (equal division required unless court finds this to be inequitable)

NORTH DAKOTA

Grounds:

(a) Felony conviction or imprisonment

(b) Drug addiction for one year

(c) Irreconcilable differences

(d) Adultery

(e) Extreme cruelty

(f) Willful desertion or willful neglect

(g) Insanity for five years

Property Distribution: Equitable Distribution

OHIO

Grounds:

(a) Bigamy

(b) Two years' separation or absence

(c) Felony conviction or imprisonment

(d) Joint bill (parties execute separation agreement and reaffirm agreement in court)

(e) Willful absence for one year

(f) Adultery

(g) Impotency

(h) Extreme cruelty

(i) Any gross neglect of duty

    (j) Habitual drunkenness
    (k) Four-year confinement in a mental insti-
        tution
Property Distribution: Equitable Distribution

OKLAHOMA
Grounds: (a) Felony conviction or imprisonment
          (b) Fraud, force or duress
          (c) Incompatibility
          (d) Adultery
          (e) Abandonment
          (f) Cruelty
          (g) Drunkenness
          (h) Insanity
          (i) Neglect of duty
Property Distribution: Equitable Distribution

OREGON
Grounds: (a) Irretrievable breakdown
Property Distribution: Equitable Distribution

PENNSYLVANIA
Grounds: (a) Bigamy
          (b) Three-year separation or absence
          (c) Felony conviction or imprisonment of two
              years
          (d) Irretrievable breakdown
          (e) Desertion without reasonable cause for at
              least one year
          (f) Adultery
          (g) Cruel and barbarous treatment
          (h) Personal indignities rendering condition
              intolerable and life burdensome
          (i) Insanity or serious mental disorder with at
              least three-year confinement
Property Distribution: Equitable Distribution

RHODE ISLAND
Grounds: (a) Bigamy
          (b) Three years' separation or absence
          (c) Drug addiction for one year
          (d) Irretrievable breakdown
          (e) Lack of capacity to consent to marriage

  (f) Impotency
  (g) Adultery
  (h) Extreme cruelty
  (i) Willful desertion for five years
  (j) Habitual drunkenness or drug addiction
Property Distribution: Equitable Distribution

SOUTH CAROLINA
  Grounds: (a) Separation or absence of one year
           (b) Drug addiction
           (c) Adultery
           (d) Physical cruelty
Property Distribution: Equitable Distribution

SOUTH DAKOTA
  Grounds: (a) One-year separation or absence
           (b) Felony conviction or imprisonment
           (c) Fraud, force or duress
           (d) Adultery
           (e) Extreme cruelty
           (f) Willful neglect or desertion
           (g) Habitual intemperance
Property Distribution: Equitable Distribution

TENNESSEE
  Grounds: (a) Bigamy
           (b) Felony conviction or imprisonment
           (c) Drug addiction
           (d) Infamous crime
           (e) Impotency
           (f) Adultery
           (g) Willful desertion without reasonable cause
           (h) Attempted murder of spouse by poison or
               other means of showing malice
           (i) Wife's pregnancy at time of marriage by
               another person without husband's knowl-
               edge
           (j) Habitual drunkenness or drug abuse
           (k) Irretrievable breakdown characterized by
               separation
           (l) Mutual consent divorce
Property Distribution: Equitable Distribution

TEXAS

Grounds:
- (a) Three years' separation or absence
- (b) Felony conviction or imprisonment
- (c) Irretrievable breakdown
- (d) Incompatibility
- (e) Insanity (requires two-year residence)
- (f) Non-support despite ability to do so
- (g) Cruelty
- (h) Adultery

Property Distribution: Community Property

UTAH

Grounds:
- (a) Separation or absence (three years with decree)
- (b) Felony conviction or imprisonment
- (c) Drug addiction
- (d) Impotency
- (e) Adultery
- (f) Willful desertion for more than one year
- (g) Habitual drunkenness
- (h) Cruel physical and mental treatment
- (i) Permanent insanity

Property Distribution: Equitable Distribution

VERMONT

Grounds:
- (a) Adultery
- (b) Intolerable severity
- (c) Willful desertion for seven years
- (d) Incurable insanity
- (e) Living apart for six months

Property Distribution: Equitable Distribution

VIRGINIA

Grounds:
- (a) One-year separation or absence
- (b) Felony conviction or imprisonment
- (c) Adultery
- (d) Cruelty
- (e) Willful desertion

Property Distribution: Title State

WASHINGTON

Grounds:
- (a) Irretrievable breakdown
- (b) Incompatibility
- (c) Living separate and apart for five years

    (d) Cruelty or personal indignities
    (e) Adultery
    (f) Intemperance
    (g) Insanity
    (h) Non-support
    (i) Abandonment
Property Distribution: Community Property

WEST VIRGINIA
Grounds: (a) Two years' separation or absence
    (b) Felony conviction or imprisonment
    (c) Drug addiction
    (d) Fraud, force or duress
    (e) Adultery
    (f) Willful abandonment for six months
    (g) Cruel and inhuman treatment
    (h) Habitual drunkenness
    (i) Permanent and incurable insanity
    (j) Abuse or neglect of a child
    (k) Irreconcilable differences
Property Distribution: Title State

WISCONSIN
Grounds: (a) Irretrievable breakdown
Property Distribution: Equitable Distribution

WYOMING
Grounds: (a) Irreconcilable differences
    (b) Incurable insanity
Property Distribution: Equitable Distribution

DISTRICT OF COLUMBIA
Grounds: (a) Separation, voluntary (six months) or involuntary (one year)
Property Distribution: Equitable Distribution

INDEX

Nebraska, divorce laws in, 185
necessaries doctrine, 64–65
  changing view of, 64
  husband's obligations in, 64
negotiators, 87
Nevada, divorce laws in, 185
New Hampshire, divorce laws
  in, 185–86
New Jersey, divorce laws in,
  186
New Mexico, divorce laws in,
  186
New York:
  divorce laws in, 186
  grounds for divorce in, 86,
    121–22
  interspousal rape charges in,
    42–43
  marital property defined by,
    26
  professional licenses and, 142
North Carolina, divorce laws
  in, 187
North Dakota, divorce laws in,
  187
notice for discovery, 112–13
notice or order for a medical
  examination, 113
notice to produce, 112–13

Ohio:
  divorce laws in, 187
  professional licenses and, 142
Oklahoma:
  divorce laws in, 188
  professional licenses and, 142
open discussions, 65–69
  attorneys and, 66–67
  benefits of, 66
  compromise and, 66
  focus of, 65
  guidelines for, 68
  permanent decisions and, 66
  realistic assessment of ex-
    penses and, 68–69
open panel plan, 90
order of ejectment, 41
order of protection, 40–46
  benefits of, 44
  description of, 40

for family, 43–44
interspousal rape and, 42–43
language of, 45
order of ejectment and, 41
permanent, 41, 42
police and, 40, 44, 46
procedure for, 40–41
temper tantrums and, 41
temporary, 40, 42
threats and, 41–42, 45–46
against wife, 44, 45–46
order of publication, 106
order of sequestration, 81
Oregon, divorce laws in, 188
Orr v. Orr, 145
out-of-court settlements,
  159–65
  advantages of, 159–60
  as fair and reasonable,
    160–62
  guidelines for acceptance of,
    162–63
  modification of, 164
  as part of divorce decree, 160
  rejection of offer in, 163
  restrictions of, 160–62
  trial beginning and, 164–65
  unilateral modification of,
    164
  validity of, 160
  winning and, 160
overdraft privileges, 37–38
ownership:
  in businesses, 138–39
  of homes, 17–26, 133–35
  rights, 133, 135

paintings, 27
paralegals, 91
payroll deduction orders, 77–78
  modification of, 78
penalty, 131
Pennsylvania, divorce laws in,
  188
pension plans, 137–38
  federal, 138
  matured rights in, 137
  military, 138
  vested rights in, 137